# What Others Are Saying About *THE INVITATION*

Jesus is the most remarkable person you will ever know. I encourage you to accept this invitation and learn more about who he is and how he can bring purpose and meaning to your life.

—Bill Pollard, Chairman Emeritus,
The Servicemaster Company

Asking about Jesus and learning what he can mean to me, to us—what a privilege! I read *THE INVITATION* with pleasure, and I congratulate Dannemiller and Stubbs on fine work. I look forward to the remaining four volumes in the Living Dialogue Series.

—Louis Weeks, Ph.D. President and Professor Emeritus,
Union–PSCE in Richmond & Charlotte

# THE INVITATION

*in dialogue with Jesus*

*as we know him in the Gospel of Mark*

JOHN DANNEMILLER + IRVING STUBBS

credo
house publishers

We invite you to join in on a journey with Jesus, the Anointed One, and with those who knew him. Join this journey and you will know him, too. If you know him already, you will get to know him better.

A fellow by the name of John Mark will be our guide. Invite friends to join you on this journey and you may share a transformational experience together. This is *THE INVITATION* of a lifetime.

***Do not let your happiness depend on something you may lose.***

**—C.S. Lewis**

*The Invitation*

P.O. Box 15007–Richmond, VA 23227



Published in the United States by Credo House Publishers,
a division of Credo Communications, LLC, Grand Rapids, Michigan.
www.credocommunications.net

ISBN-13: 978-1-935391-28-9
ISBN-10: 1-935391-28-3



Cover and interior design: Design Corps, Batavia, IL (designcorps.us)
Interior layout: Virginia McFadden

14 13 12 11 10 09     7 6 5 4 3 2 1
*Printed in the United States of America*

# ACKNOWLEDGMENTS

**Many people** helped us refine this book. Some participated in dialogue sessions; many gave us suggestions for improving the book; some helped us with production steps. With gratitude we list these contributors: Amy Bailey, Joan and Tom Cochran, Nancy and Russ Cooley, Candy Grooms, Bill King, Daryl Donovan, Duanne and Tim MacMillan, Brian Regrut, Rick Shaw, Alice and Ron Windahl, Joan Winter.

**Special thanks** to Jean Dannemiller for her contributions to the book and for her patience and understanding about all the time the project has taken from Jack's family activities. **And** special thanks to Ann Stubbs who encouraged Irving to work on this project, read and gave feedback on all versions of the manuscript, and who gave up Irving's time spent in his office and away from home on this mission.

The authors acknowledge indebtedness to our publishing team that includes project director Dirk Wierenga, editor Scott Philip Stewart, and attorney/partner Henry R. Pollard, IV. Our team shares the conviction that serious participants in our engagement of the soul of the Bible will experience liberating Truth for their lives.

For more than a decade, the authors were closely associated with the senior executives of Applied Industrial Technologies. We used dialogue to deal with critical business issues. That experience was a model for the learning, stretching, and relating that we covet for those who use this book. We are grateful to that group of dedicated leaders.

We are eternally grateful for our experience with Jesus, the Messiah. For us, he is the liberator, the light of our life's journey, and the One whose acceptance of us is the source of our transformation. He gives us the courage to be what God calls us to be. In thanksgiving for the gifts he has given us, we are challenged to serve him by serving others.

## KEY QUESTIONS FOR YOUR JOURNEY

What was Jesus' mission?
Who did he include in his mission?
How did he want his mission to continue?
Are you ready to participate in that mission?

# CONTENTS

# INTRODUCTION

If you were given the chance to engage in serious dialogue with anyone who ever lived on planet earth, who would you choose? Think about it. It could be anybody—maybe Elvis or Joan of Arc, maybe Marie Antoinette or Michelangelo . . . or Jesus.

In survey after survey, more people choose Jesus Christ than anyone else.

In this book we hope to encourage what is perhaps the next best thing to an actual face-to-face dialogue with Jesus—we invite you to *take a journey with Jesus*. Your tour guide will be Mark, a contemporary of Jesus who wrote the Gospel of Mark. Mark does not attempt to interpret Jesus. He takes a "just the facts" approach in his gospel, or story, about Jesus. He lets us walk with Jesus, eavesdrop on his conversations, and listen in on his teachings. But in the end he leaves it up to us to decide what to make of Jesus.

So in *The Invitation* Jesus is presented without interpretation. You are challenged to find your own interpretation. We do not focus on what is thought *about* Jesus. We focus on getting to know Jesus and relating to him.

So we invite you to lay aside all preconceptions and popular notions about Jesus and engage in a dialogue with him to discover who he really is.

### Who is *THE INVITATION* for?

For anyone who would like to know Jesus better or who thinks Jesus is someone *worth* getting to know better. Those who have questions about what they have heard about Jesus and those with questions they would like to ask him will find it especially interesting—and challenging.

**What's the best way to take this journey?**

We encourage getting to know Jesus better and relating to him in the context of a type of transforming conversation—what we call dialogue. Despite all the high-tech devices we have for communicating in our day—landlines and cell phones, Blackberries and PDAs, email and teleconferencing—our communication is shallow. "Talking points" are dull and "sound bites" are not filling. "Chatting" has replaced heart-to-heart talks, and so many of us are conditioned to skim along the surface of ideas and events without discovering the profound truths that lie deep inside the experience.

So we want to encourage dialogue on the journey. Few of us like to travel alone. Experiences are richer when they are shared. If you took a trip to some exotic locale and saw things the likes of which you had never seen, wouldn't you want to tell somebody about it? Better yet, wouldn't you like to have somebody along to share the *"Wow!"*?

So in your small group of traveling companions, you can share the experiences through dialogue. If you associate the word "dialogue" with some dull and boring academic discipline, we invite you to a different understanding of the word. Dialogue is the opposite of small talk: It is "big" talk, a heart-to-heart sharing that has the power to transform both parties to the "transforming conversation."

**Eavesdropping on Jesus' dialogue with his disciples**

In this book you will be listening in on the dialogue Jesus had with his followers and others. As you do, put yourself in their shoes. Listen to their voices (they might just echo some of your own thoughts). Then go beyond simply listening and become part of the dialogue. For dialogue can change your life.

**Dialogues**

We believe that God calls each of us to a personal relationship with him—a relationship that gives meaning and purpose to our lives. God wants deep, personal, and open communication with us. We see this as our *spiritual* ***dialogue with God***.

So as you eavesdrop on Jesus' conversations and spy on the events of his life, you may experience thoughts and feelings that clarify, stretch, and challenge your understanding of Jesus. This will be *an internal* ***dialogue with your self***. You might think, "I never thought about it that way." "Did he really say that?" "I wonder what he meant by *that*?"

Recording your personal impressions can expand your perspective and your understanding of yourself. Each segment of the book has space for you to record your internal dialogue. This can be a travel log of your relationship with Jesus.

You may also exchange thoughts and feelings with family members, friends, or coworkers that amplify and deepen your understanding of Jesus. This will be ***dialogue with others who are physically present***. Some of us hear messages from Jesus in the words of others. Some of us have dialogues with Jesus in the quiet moments of life. These are *dialogues* ***with another, not present physically*** *but present spiritually*.

**About our travel log—the Gospel of Mark**

When Jesus was on earth he favored dialogue as the preferred way of relating to others—friends and enemies alike. In the decades after his time on earth was over, no written account of the life and work of Jesus was available. The earliest believers had no New Testament to which they could turn to learn about him, no

Bible commentaries, no biographies, no motion pictures. What they did have is dialogue, and in small groups they would gather and share their thoughts and impressions about what they had heard and what each of them thought it meant.

So when Mark wrote his account of Jesus' ministry, he did so in a way that captured Jesus' own preferred way of relating—dialogue, transforming conversation, asking questions. One *New Testament* scholar had this to say about Jesus' questioning in the Gospel of Mark:

"This is more than a simple device of the tradition, or of Mark, to convey vividness by dialogue; such a characteristic, quasi-Socratic style, must go back to Jesus himself. As a good teacher and pastor he encouraged others to express their wishes, hopes, aspirations and gave opportunity to them to express their faith, upon which he could then act and build."[1]

That is the essence of dialogue—encouraging one another to express our wishes, hopes, and aspirations and to express our faith! Jesus built relationships with his friends through encouraging dialogue. Through it he offers a life of love, purpose, joy, and the courage to respond to the uncertainties of life that each of us experiences. He gives us good reasons to greet each day with excitement and anticipation. And he also gives us the courage and faith to deal with the inevitable end of our life's journey on planet earth.

Dialogue—transforming conversation—helps us to understand and trust each other and to find truth together. As you engage and respond to the content of this book in dialogue with yourself, Jesus, and others, you can shift from merely looking at the good news reported here to living that good news.

So in using dialogue to get to know Jesus we are using his own preferred way of communicating. Early Christians shaped their faith by asking questions. They listened for what made sense to them. They applied the truth to their lives to confirm their faith by experience. In their search, they found clarity as new information and experience provided a convincing basis for their faith.

An appendix offers information about dialogue that will help you get the most out of your group. Take these guidelines to heart. This type of transforming conversation is only a "mystery" to those who have never experienced it. This was the way Jesus taught and it can positively revolutionize your communication with God and with others in your life.

**Invitation to a Unique Way of Life**

Mark's presentation of Jesus discloses a unique way of life, which will become clearer to you as you interact with this book. We do not reference chapters and verses of the Gospel in the book. We ask you to focus not on the pieces of the puzzle but on the picture as a whole.

We do not presume to tell you what your response to Jesus Christ should be. We focus on what Jesus said to various individuals, groups, and large crowds. We present short but significant moments in his three-year ministry and encourage you to share their impact on you with others in your dialogue group.

The first ten chapters of Mark's Gospel (Segments 1-30) report the ministry of Jesus. The last six (Segments 31-52) report what Jesus experienced to reveal God's love and the sacrifice involved in our redemption and renewal. You may hear from Jesus through your mind (intellect), your heart (emotions), and your conscience. You may ask, "How does this apply to my life?"

J. Middleton Murry said in *Jesus–Man of Genius*:

"The time had come when it had become urgent upon me to make up my mind about Jesus." [2]

Mary Ely Lyman in her book *Jesus* wrote:

"This compulsion comes to most thinking people. One must reckon with a life that has made so much difference to all succeeding history. One must think of it not merely historically, but from the point of view of his meaning for us."[3]

Where it seemed appropriate to illuminate the context of an incident in the life of Jesus we have drawn on various Bible commentaries. We have deliberately avoided "editorializing" on the events and were content to let them stand alone without interpretation. We encourage you, however, to do your own interpreting. If you suspend previous understandings of Jesus and let Mark focus you on Jesus as his Gospel reveals him, you may experience a fresh and more personal encounter with Jesus, his mission, and his message.

*The Gospel of Mark* is the shortest and probably the earliest written of the four Gospels. Although the earliest available draft of the Gospel bears no author's name, many scholars agree that it was John Mark. Most likely he was Jewish but he had a Roman name (Mark). William Barclay [4] reported that Mark was the son of a well-to-do lady of Jerusalem whose house was a meeting place for early Christians.

Mark grew up in the center of that early Christian fellowship and knew the early leaders of the Church. He was the nephew of Barnabas, who traveled with the Apostle Paul on his first missionary journey. Mark was an associate of the Apostle Peter (*apostle* means "one who is sent"), who was beheaded about 60–65 A.D.

Mark probably wrote his Gospel in Rome during the middle decades of the first century. Jews had lived in Rome for over a century and were one of the largest foreign blocs in that city. Jewish Christians often found themselves in conflict with Roman authorities with respect to their beliefs, their practices, and their loyalties. Nero the Roman emperor, for instance, blamed Christians for setting Rome on fire. Many were persecuted.

Mark wrote primarily to Gentile (non-Jewish) Christians, to those who, as Frederick C. Grant viewed it, "may be called to enter the arena with its hungry wild beasts or be coated with tar and strung up and ignited as living torches in Nero's gardens."[5] Mark was familiar with their struggles and wrote for those who had survived this holocaust and lost their leaders and were living in a very hostile environment. They were under pressure from both Jews *and* pagans for their faith. Mark sought to encourage Gentile Christians by telling what he knew about Jesus. Mark's story reaches a climax in the death of Jesus on the cross. Early Christians found courage in Jesus' willingness to be crucified.

Although probably 40 years elapsed between the end of Jesus' life on earth and the writing of this Gospel, it is likely that Peter's eyewitness experience was Mark's primary source. Eyewitnesses to the life of Jesus told their stories about Jesus and the impact he had in the Hebrew or Aramaic languages. Mark recorded these stories by hand in Greek as depicted in the manuscript shown on the next page.

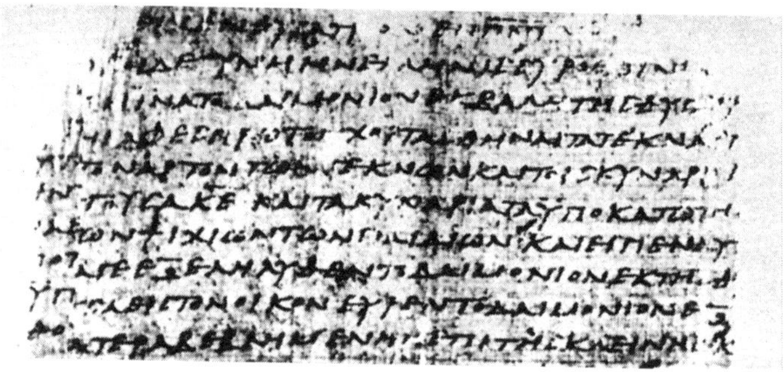

**Lines in Greek from *the Gospel of Mark* from the Chester Beatty papyrus from the third century.**

—Emery Walker, Ltd. London—from *The Pictorial Gospel of Mark* [6]

English translations of Mark's Gospel are based on multiple manuscripts (similar to the one pictured above) and were circulated in the early Christian church. There are many times more copies of biblical manuscripts than any other ancient historical books, so we can trust that *The Gospel of Mark* has deep roots and accept it as an authentic witness to the life and teachings of Jesus.

**How the *Gospel of Mark* Begins**

*The Gospel of Mark* begins with the preaching of John the baptizer, a wild rustic man who spent most of his time in the wilderness. He dined on locusts and wild honey and wore camel-hair clothes. He believed himself to be God's messenger whose mission was to prepare the way for Jesus. John called people to repent: to confess their sins and choose to change. Repent means to have a profound change of mind, a change of the inner view of reality, a turning of the will in a new direction, and a revamped purpose for living.

JOHN THE BAPTIST PREACHING IN THE WILDERNESS

For their cleansing and renewal, John baptized people in the Jordan River. He told them that his baptism was with water but that the Lord who would come after him would baptize with the Holy Spirit. One day, Jesus from Nazareth made his way out to the Jordan and asked John to baptize him. John said, in effect, "I'm not worthy," but he baptized him anyway. When he did a voice from heaven declared Jesus to be the beloved Son of God.

After his baptism, Jesus spent 40 days praying and fasting in the wilderness where Satan came and tempted him. Then Jesus visited the region of Galilee proclaiming that the kingdom of God was at hand and urging all to repent and believe this good news.

The whole story of Jesus told in the Gospel of Mark takes place in a country the size of the state of New Jersey over a period of just three years, "but its meaning is infinite."[7] The whole account is closer in length to a short story than to a novel. But this short story changed history, humankind, and the societies in which we live. It was well described as *The Greatest Story Ever Told.* The "good news" of this story changes all who believe in it. This life-changing "good news" is what the Gospel of Mark is all about.

*Note:* Refer to the maps on pages 68–71 to journey with Jesus geographically as well as with his words and spirit.

**CHAPTER ONE**

# ON THE SHORES OF THE SEA OF GALILEE

## *Segments 1-11*

Many things happened on and around the Sea of Galilee, which was a lake about 13 miles long and eight miles wide fed by the Jordan River. In Jesus' day, nine towns flourished on its shores, including Capernaum at the northern end. The region of Galilee was 50 miles long and 30 miles wide and was home to 204 towns and cities.

### 1. What about Jesus?

Jesus chose to carry out his ministry through a small group of men he called "disciples" (which literally means "learners"). One day when he was about 30 years old, while strolling along the shores of the Sea of Galilee, Jesus spotted two brothers, Simon and Andrew. They were fishermen at work casting their nets into the sea. "*Come, follow me,*" Jesus said to them, "*and I will make you fishers of men.*" They dropped everything—including their nets—and immediately followed Jesus. A little later, Jesus saw another pair of fishermen brothers, James and John, who were in a boat with their father and some others. He called them, too. And they responded by leaving everything—including their father—and followed him.

## DIALOGUE

1. *Has there been a time in your life when you have "dropped everything" or "left everything" for someone or something? Do you know someone else who has?*

2. *Can you imagine what might make you "drop everything" and follow a stranger? What would it take to get you out of the boat (or your office, or home, or comfort zone...)?*

3. *Jesus lured these fishermen to follow him. What "bait" do you think could have led these men to "immediately" respond to the call of a perfect stranger?*

4. *Put yourself in their position—minding their own business, going about their daily work. Under what circumstances would a person say* **yes** *to such a call?*

5. *Do you think there was something about Jesus that attracted them? What might that have been? What about Jesus would make you willing to accept his invitation to follow him?*

6. *What does Jesus' play on words "fishers of men" mean to you?*

7. *How can you relate this experience to your own life's journey?*

### GROUP DIALOGUE POWER TIP

To lay the groundwork for the dialogue group, the leader should define the purpose and parameters of the dialogue and share the guidelines for effective dialogue.

The intention is:

*Not to advocate but to inquire*

*Not to argue but to explore*

*Not to convince but to discover*

—Louise Diamond [8]

## JOURNAL

## 2. What qualities did Jesus display?

Jesus and his new followers went to a town called Capernaum. On Saturday (the seventh day of the week called the Sabbath, which was set aside for rest and devotion), they entered the synagogue. At that time a synagogue was a place of assembly where people met for prayer, scripture study, and community gatherings. Jesus rose and taught the assembly. A man with an evil spirit came into the synagogue and cried out, *"What do you want with us, Jesus of Nazareth? Have you come to destroy us? I know who you are—the Holy One of God."* Jesus responded, *"Be quiet! Come out of him."* The unclean spirit convulsed the man and came out of him. Those present in the synagogue were amazed and said among themselves, *"What is this? A new teaching—and with authority! He even gives orders to evil spirits, and they obey him."*

JESUS PREACHES AT THE SYNAGOGUE

After they left the synagogue, Jesus, James, and John went to the home of Simon Peter and Andrew. Simon Peter's mother-in-law was sick with a fever, so Jesus took her hand and helped her up. The fever left her and she served them.

That evening, people brought to Jesus many who were sick or possessed with demons. As if summoned to some great celebration, all the people of the town gathered at Peter and Andrew's front door. And Jesus, as the master of ceremonies, healed many with various diseases and cast out many demons.

## DIALOGUE

1. *Picture yourself sitting in church when in walks a guest speaker and begins teaching. Then a person suffering from some serious mental illness comes in. The guest speaker heals the person right then and there. How do you think you might react? What thoughts might run through your mind?*

2. *Continuing with question 1: Let's say a loved one (a parent, child, or spouse) is suffering from a serious mental or physical illness, would you take that person to Jesus?*

3. *Do you think that what they used to call "unclean spirits" or "demon possession" exist in our own day? If so, explain.*

4. *Why do you think Jesus chose to begin his ministry with healings?*

5. *Do you know anyone who has been healed of a disease—mental or physical? Have you ever witnessed a "miracle"? Do you think some Christians today have the power to heal?*

6. *What qualities did Jesus display in these miracles?*

7. *How can you relate this experience to your own life's journey?*

## JOURNAL

3. unclean spirits - mental illness
2. they nothing ventured nothing gained

4- to get attention, set himself apart from other itinerant preachers, as proof he was what he said he was.

**3. How did Jesus perceive himself?**

News about his authoritative teaching and wonderworking began spreading, and before long Jesus had become a celebrity. Great crowds greeted him wherever he went. A few days after he had healed the man with the evil spirit in the synagogue, Jesus returned to Capernaum. Word spread that he was back home and people swarmed to the house and gathered out in the yard. Four men attempted to carry a paralyzed man to him in hopes that Jesus would heal him. There was not even standing room to get close to Jesus, so they carried the pallet-ridden man up on the roof, opened a hole, and lowered him down into the house.

When Jesus saw their faith, he said to the paralyzed man, *"Son, your sins are forgiven."* Not everyone in the crowd took this as good news, though. Some scribes, experts in the law of Moses (who were the official Bible teachers of the day), considered what Jesus said as blasphemy because they believed that only God could forgive sins. Jesus answered the charge: *"Which is easier to say to the paralytic, 'Your sins are forgiven,' or 'Get up, take your mat and walk?'"* Then he turned to the paralyzed man and said, *"Rise, take up your pallet and go home."* The man rose, took up his pallet, and left.

Amazed, those in the crowd said, *"We have never seen anything like this!"*

## DIALOGUE

1. ***What does this event tell us about how Jesus saw himself?***

2. ***How did the crowd see Jesus? Was their opinion about him unanimous? Are people's opinions about Jesus unanimous in our day?***

3. ***What impressed Jesus about the four men who brought their paralyzed friend to him?***

4. ***What does their reaction to the event tell us about the Scribes—teachers of the law?***

5. ***What do you think Jesus meant when he asked the scribes which was easier—to tell the paralyzed man that his sins were forgiven or to tell him to get up and walk?***

6. ***What do you think they concluded from what Jesus said and did?***

7. ***How can you relate this experience to your own life's journey?***

## JOURNAL

### 4. How did Jesus view the religious practices of his day?

Jesus returned to the shores of the Sea of Galilee. He saw a man named Levi sitting in the tax office and said to him, "*Follow me.*" Levi, a tax collector, followed Jesus. In those days, the job of tax collector was granted to the highest bidder. Why would someone bid for a job? Because a tax collector could charge whatever tax he wanted to cover—and exceed—his investment. The Jews in Jesus' day had to pay one third of their income for taxes. It is no wonder that tax collectors were unpopular. Because they were agents of the Roman Empire, many considered tax collectors to be traitors willing to sell out Israel to the Roman overlords.

So when Jesus and his followers accepted Levi's invitation to dine in his home, certain scribes of a group called Pharisees questioned Jesus' judgment. How dare he—a "religious leader"—dine with tax collectors and sinners. Pharisees were themselves religious leaders who held the Jewish laws to be the sum of religion and to govern every aspect of life. Jesus' response to the scribes' concern was: "*It is not the healthy who need a doctor, but the sick. I have not come to call the righteous, but sinners.*"

The followers of John the baptizer and the followers of the Pharisees practiced fasting. The followers of Jesus did not. This led some to ask Jesus why his disciples did not follow these practices. Jesus replied: "*How can the guests of the bridegroom fast while he is with them? They cannot so long as they have him with them. But the time will come when the bridegroom will be taken from them, and on that day they will fast.*"

## DIALOGUE

1. ***It is hard to come up with a parallel for Jesus' call of Levi the tax collector. We might liken it to a well-known Christian evangelist in our own day who calls an equally well-known but notorious gangster to join him in ministry. Think about it. What would people say? Would they respond as the scribes and the Pharisees did in Jesus' day?***

2. ***What do you find most striking about the calling of Levi the tax collector? What is your takeaway from the encounter?***

3. ***Put yourself in Levi's place. How do you think you would feel about Jesus' invitation?***

4. ***What do the facts that Jesus was willing to eat with tax collectors and sinners and did not require his followers to practice ritual fasting suggest about Jesus' view of religious practices?***

5. ***Do you think that Jesus' views about religious practices might unsettle some religious leaders today? How?***

6. *Have you ever sensed a call from Jesus to you? If so, how did you respond?*

7. *How can you relate this experience to your own life's journey?*

## JOURNAL

________________________________________

________________________________________

________________________________________

________________________________________

________________________________________

________________________________________

________________________________________

________________________________________

________________________________________

### 5. Why did the Pharisees want to destroy Jesus?

One Sabbath day as they walked through a grain field, Jesus' followers plucked some heads of grain. The Pharisees (who never let Jesus stray too far from view) challenged Jesus: *"Look, why are they doing what is unlawful on the Sabbath?"* Jesus answered: *"Have you never read what David did, when he and his companions were hungry and in need? ... He entered the house of God and ate the consecrated bread, which is lawful for only priests to eat. ... The Sabbath was made for man, not man for the Sabbath. So the Son of man is Lord even of the Sabbath."*

A short time later, the Pharisees spied Jesus in the synagogue interacting with a man who had a shriveled hand. *Would he dare heal the man on the Sabbath and, in so doing, break the law?* Jesus invited the man with the shriveled hand to come to him. He asked the Pharisees, *"Which is lawful on the Sabbath: to do good or to do evil, to save life or to kill?"* The Pharisees were silent. Jesus looked at them and bristled, grieved at their hardness of heart. Then he said to the man, *"Stretch out your hand."* The man stretched out his hand, and it was completely restored.

The Pharisees left and went to plot with the Herodians—members of a political party friendly with Herod, who claimed to be "King of the Jews," on how to destroy Jesus.

## DIALOGUE

1. ***Why do you think the Pharisees wanted to destroy Jesus? What would their motives be?***

2. ***We have a saying, "No good deed goes unpunished." How do you think that relates to the story of Jesus' healing the man on the Sabbath?***

3. ***What is the message here about religious rules?***

4. ***Have you ever seen people in our own day who "play the Pharisee" in the way they react to certain situations? Who? Why?***

5. ***What did Jesus mean when he told the Pharisees, "The Sabbath was made for man?"***

6. ***The Sabbath was a day set aside for rest. How do you observe the Sabbath? Why?***

7. ***How can you relate this experience to your own life's journey?***

## JOURNAL

### 6. Does it surprise you?

Jesus again went to the seaside. He was attracting ever larger crowds of people seeking his help. He withdrew to the hills and invited several others to follow him—and they did. He appointed 12 to be with him as an inner circle of apostles (or "messengers"), also known as disciples:

**James** and his brother **John** (whom he called *Boanerges,* meaning "thunderbolts"; fishermen by trade)
**Simon** (whom Jesus called Peter, or *Rock*) and his brother
**Andrew** (also fishermen by trade)
**Philip**
**Bartholomew**
**Levi** (also called Matthew, a tax collector)
**Thomas**
**James**, son of Alphaeus

**Thaddaeus**
**Simon** (who was a Zealot, a party that advocated the violent overthrow of Roman control of Israel)
**Judas Iscariot** (who ultimately betrayed him)

Disciples were devoted pupils who followed a leader (in those days a rabbi) and carried out and carried on the teachings and practices of the master. Jesus sent his disciples out to preach the gospel ("good news") and empowered them to cast out demons.

After calling the disciples, Jesus seized the moment to teach them a profound lesson on two topics with eternal consequences—sin and the ministry of the Holy Spirit—before he sent them out to preach. The Holy Spirit is the one who convicts people that they have broken God's laws and therefore need a savior; the Holy Spirit points people to Jesus.

Jesus said: *"I tell you the truth, all the sins and blasphemies of men will be forgiven them. But whoever blasphemes against the Holy Spirit will never be forgiven; He is guilty of an eternal sin."*

## DIALOGUE

1. ***Are you surprised that Jesus got such a ready response from the disciples he called? If so, why?***

2. ***What do you believe Jesus charged them to preach about? Does it surprise you that he gave them power to cast out demons?***

3. ***What comes to mind when you hear the word "sin"? What is your view of sin? What do you believe is God's view of sin?***

4. ***Does it surprise you that Jesus' first teaching was about sin and the Holy Spirit? Why? Why was it needed?***

5. *Does it surprise you that Jesus referred to a sin that will never be forgiven? Why?*

6. *Do you feel forgiven of all your sins? If so, why?*

7. *How can you relate this experience to your own life's journey?*

## JOURNAL

## 7. What kind of soil are you?

When news about all that Jesus was doing got back to his family, they came looking for him—suspecting that he had gone mad. They gathered with the crowd outside his house. Someone told Jesus that his mother and brothers were outside looking for him. Jesus asked them, *"Who are my mother and my brothers?"* He looked around at those who were sitting around him and said, *"Here are my mother and my brothers! Whoever does God's will is my brother and sister and mother."*

Jesus returned to the seaside and a large crowd assembled. He got into a boat and addressed the crowd. He used parables to convey his message. Parables are simple stories drawn from everyday life that reveal profound truths.

He told a parable about a farmer who went out to sow seed. *"As he was scattering the seed, some seed fell along the path, and the birds came and ate it up. Some fell on rocky places, however, where it did not have much soil. It sprang up quickly, because the soil was shallow. But when the sun came up, the plants were scorched and they withered because they had no root. Other seed fell among thorns, which grew up and choked the plants, so that they did not bear grain. Still other seed fell on good soil. It came up, grew and produced a crop, multiplying thirty, sixty or even a hundred times. He who has ears to hear, let him hear."*

## DIALOGUE

1. ***Does Jesus' response when his mother and brothers came seeking him surprise you in any way? If so, how?***

2. ***What do you think Jesus meant when he said that whoever does God's will is his brother and sister and mother?***

3. ***What do you think it means to "do God's will"? Can you think of anyone today whom you would say is doing God's will? Who? Why?***

4. ***As you apply the parable of the farmer to your own life, what kind of soil are you—(a) path (no soil), (b) little soil (rocky places), (c) shallow, or (d) good (rich soil)? What do you base your answer on?***

5. ***What do you think the thorns that choke plants represent in the parable? Can you identify any thorns in your own life?***

*6. What would you consider to be a good "yield" from your life?*

*7. How can you relate this experience to your own life's journey?*

**GROUP DIALOGUE POWER TIP**

Benefits for group participants:

- Enjoyed exchange of ideas—good mental stimulation
- Small groups give courage to share ideas, to speak and be heard
- Questions stimulate new thought

## JOURNAL

**8. How do you connect your light and your faith?**

Jesus continued his teaching. "*Do you bring in a lamp to put it under a bowl or a bed? Instead, don't you put it on its stand? For whatever is hidden is meant to be discovered, and whatever is concealed is meant to be brought out into the open. With the measure*

JESUS STILLING THE TEMPEST

*you use, it will be measured to you—and even more. Whoever has will be given more; whoever does not have, even what he has will be taken from him."*

That evening, as they were crossing the Sea of Galilee, a furious squall came up and whipped the sea into a choppy froth. Waves broke over the rails and the boat began taking on water. All the while Jesus was in the back of the boat sound asleep. Terrified, the disciples woke Jesus up and asked if he cared that they were going to die. Jesus calmed the storm and said to them, *"Why are you still afraid? Do you still have no faith?"*

## DIALOGUE

1. ***What do you think Jesus was getting at when he said that lamps should be placed on stands not under baskets?***

2. ***What does the light represent in your life? Are you hiding any light in your own life?***

3. ***What is the lesson here about making wise use of God's resources?***

4. ***Has there been a time in your life when you were afraid that something terrible was going to happen or that you were going to die? Describe that experience.***

5. ***What did that fear do to you? What did you do to relieve or overcome that fear?***

6. ***What do you think Jesus meant when he related "fear" to "lack of faith"?***

7. ***How can you relate this experience to your own life's journey?***

## JOURNAL

### 9. What have you learned about Jesus?

On the other side of the sea, they came to the country of the Gerasenes. A violent man with evil spirits came out from among the tombs to meet them. The man was what we might call a "hard case"; he was too mighty to be controlled and had busted out of the restraints that bound him—restraints made of iron and chain. He shouted wildly and bruised himself with stones. But when he saw Jesus, the man ran to him and worshipped him and begged him not to torment him. Jesus asked his name. *"Legion,"* he replied (because he was possessed with many "demons"). A herd of about 2,000 pigs was feeding on the hillside. Jesus gave the evil spirits permission to enter the pigs, and they left the man and entered the pigs. The pigs rushed down the bank into the sea and drowned. Those attending the pigs ran off and told people in the city what had happened.

When they heard such a wild tale, many went to see the spectacle and the one who had caused it for themselves. *How could this wild man be tamed?* What they saw was Jesus sitting there with the madman—only now he was calm and in his right mind. They begged Jesus to leave their neighborhood. As Jesus and his disciples were getting into the boat, the demoniac begged them to let him come along. Jesus instructed him instead to go and tell his friends how much the Lord had done for him. The man accepted the challenge, and those who heard him were amazed.

## DIALOGUE

1. ***What does this episode add to what you have learned about Jesus? What aspects of the story struck you as peculiar or unexpected?***

2. ***Put yourself in the place of those who came out and saw the madman (who lived in the tombs and snapped his leg irons!) sitting there calm and rational. What thoughts might go through your mind? Have you ever experienced anything at all like this?***

3. ***If you were one of Jesus' disciples and the herdsman complained to you about the loss of his swine, what would you say to him?***

4. ***Why did the Gerasenes beg Jesus to leave their neighborhood?***

5. ***Why did Jesus deny the man's request to join his disciples?***

6. ***How have you responded to the challenges given you by Jesus? Are you telling friends what God has done for you? If not, why not?***

7. ***How can you relate this experience to your own life's journey?***

## JOURNAL

## 10. What about Jairus?

Jesus and his disciples returned to the other side of the sea where again a great crowd awaited them. A man named Jairus, one of the leaders of the Jewish synagogue (who led the worship services), fell at Jesus' feet and pleaded earnestly with him: "*My little daughter is dying. Please come and put your hands on her so that she will be healed and live.*"

While he was speaking, word came to Jairus that his daughter had died. Jesus said to Jairus, "*Don't be afraid; just believe.*" Jesus took only Peter, James, and John with him to Jairus' house. When they got there, they found a sad commotion with people weeping and wailing. Jesus entered the house and announced: "*The child is not dead but asleep.*" They laughed at these words—such nonsense! But Jesus took the child's father and mother and the disciples and went in to the little girl and took her hand and said, "*Little girl, I say to you, get up!*" Immediately, she got up and walked. He told them to give her something to eat. Those present were overcome with amazement. In this case, Jesus strictly charged them that no one should know this.

### DIALOGUE

1. *Did you learn anything new about Jesus from this event? If so, what?*

2. *Are you surprised that Jairus, a worship service leader, would come to Jesus with his plea? Why or why not?*

3. *Why do you suppose Jairus believed that Jesus could heal his daughter?*

4. *Why do you think Jesus did not want anyone else to know about this?*

5. *The word "immediately" occurs 41 times in the Gospel of Mark. What do you make of this? When you hear the word "immediately" how does it strike you?*

6. *Do you feel any sense of urgency about your response to the invitation of Jesus to accept his Good News?*

7. *How can you relate this experience to your own life's journey?*

## JOURNAL

### 11. How would you measure your faith?

While Jesus and the others were on their way to Jairus' house, a desperate woman approached him. The woman had a flow of blood for 12 years and had suffered much under the care of many physicians. Despite having spent all she had in quest of a cure, not only was she no better but in fact had grown worse. She had nothing to lose.

*"When she heard about Jesus, she came up behind him in the crowd and touched his cloak, because she thought, 'If I just touch his clothes, I will be healed.' Immediately her bleeding stopped and she felt in her body that she was freed from her suffering."*

Jesus felt power flowing from him and asked, *"Who touched my clothes?"* The woman, realizing what had happened to her and trembling with fear, told Jesus the whole truth. *"Daughter,"* responded Jesus, *"your faith has healed you. Go in peace, and be freed from your suffering."*

### GROUP DIALOGUE POWER TIP

In groups, some members speak out and others hold back. In dialogue groups, it is important to invite those who hold back to speak out. This may require those more ready to speak out to hold back for a while to allow others to contribute. Some discipline is needed to assure equal opportunity for all members to contribute. Nevertheless, respect the personal styles of all members of the group.

## DIALOGUE

1. *Can you relate to this woman in some way? Have you ever felt as though you had exhausted all options for solving a problem in your life—as though you had nothing to lose? Have you ever sought a last resort?*

2. *Jesus took no credit for the woman's healing. Instead, he attributed her healing to her faith. So if her faith made her well, how would you describe the faith she must have had? What do you think was the source of her faith?*

3. *Do you believe that faith has the power to heal? If so, do you believe it can heal physical (medical) illnesses? Emotional problems? Relationship troubles? Spiritual dis-ease?*

4. *Some seemed to understand Jesus and others seemed unable to understand him. What enables us to understand Jesus?*

5. *If you were a reporter for* **The Jerusalem Gazette** *who was tasked with getting the scoop on Jesus, what would the highlights of your article on this event be?*

6. *How would you measure your own faith in light of faith as Jesus defined it?*

7. *How can you relate this experience to your own life's journey?*

## JOURNAL

## CHAPTER TWO

# NAZARETH

### *Segments 12-13*

**12. What if you were a neighbor of Jesus?**

Jesus returned to Nazareth—his hometown—and again went to teach in the synagogue. Many who heard him—and surely had known him all his life—wondered how he had acquired the wisdom he was teaching and the wherewithal to do what he was doing—working miracles. Their reaction swung quickly from wonder and amazement to bitterness. *"Isn't this the carpenter?"* they questioned. *"Isn't this Mary's son and the brother of James? Aren't his sisters here with us?"* And Mark says they took offense at him. Jesus said to them, *"Only in his hometown, among his relatives and in his own house is a prophet without honor."*

Nazareth was the childhood home of Jesus. He had likely lived there for 30 years before he left to begin his public ministry. Nazareth was a small town in Galilee with a population under 500. So when Jesus came back for a visit and taught in the synagogue, many who knew him as a carpenter found *him* hard to believe. How could this familiar man—a carpenter, Mary's son, James's brother, one of their own whom they had known all his life—be so different? Something was happening in his life to make him seem very different from what he had been before.

## DIALOGUE

1. *Why do you think those who knew Jesus and his family were unable to accept him as he was now expressing himself?*

2. *Have you known of a hometown boy or girl who "made good" or made it to the "big time"? How did people respond to the change? How did you respond to the change? Was it hard to believe?*

3. *If you were a neighbor and friend of Jesus' family, what might you ask them at this turning point in Jesus' life?*

4. *If you had a profound, life-transforming religious experience, would it be easier to share this with your family and neighbors or with total strangers? Why, or why not?*

5. *Have you ever found it difficult to share your faith with others? If so, try to pinpoint some of the reasons. What would make it easier to share your religious experience and faith with others?*

6. *During much of his life, Jesus seemed not to seek recognition and acceptance by the general public. Based on our journey thus far, on what basis do you think Jesus wanted to be recognized and accepted?*

7. *How can you relate this experience to your own life's journey?*

### GROUP DIALOGUE POWER TIP

Instead of listening to determine what is correct or to find agreement, it is important to listen to find what is *meant*. What does the person who is speaking *mean*?

## JOURNAL

### 13. How are hearers to repent?

Shortly after leaving Nazareth, Jesus turned his attention to extending his mission through his disciples. He sent them out in pairs and empowered them to represent him—preaching the need for repentance (change of heart), driving out demons, and healing the sick. He instructed them to travel light (no bread, no money, no extra coat) and stay with those who received them. *"And if any place will not welcome you or listen to you," he told them, "shake the dust off your feet when you leave, as a testimony against them."*

News about Jesus and the ministry of his disciples spread, and King Herod, the ruler of Galilee and son of Herod the Great, caught wind of it. This is the same Herod who had ordered the beheading of John the baptizer. Rumors were circulating about just who this Jesus of Nazareth really was. Herod took him to be John the baptizer raised from the dead. Others believed that he was one of the prophets of old, perhaps Elijah.

## DIALOGUE

1. *Jesus sent the disciples out in pairs to deliver the message that people were to repent. What did he mean by that?*

2. *By that definition, have you repented? If so, how did you do it?*

3. *Jesus empowered the disciples to preach, drive out demons, and heal the sick. Do you sometimes feel empowered to represent (re-present) Jesus? If so, how?*

4. *You have listened to Jesus. You have questioned Jesus. You might have learned some things about him that you never knew. In the course of this journey, have you received any messages from Jesus? If so, what were they?*

5. *If not, can you identify anything that might hinder you from receiving messages from him?*

6. *What kind of power does Jesus give when he empowers people today?*

7. *How can you relate this experience to your own life's journey?*

## JOURNAL

## CHAPTER THREE

# A LONELY PLACE

### *Segment 14*

**14. What "hooked" Jesus to do this big thing?**

The 12 apostles returned from their mission and told Jesus all that they had experienced. Jesus invited them to retreat to a quiet place to rest for a while (for with all the bustle and coming and going, Mark says, they didn't even have a chance to eat). So they all got into a boat and headed across the sea to a deserted place. But many saw them leaving and went ahead of them on foot, so that by the time they rowed the boat ashore a great crowd had assembled. *When Jesus landed and saw a large crowd, he had compassion on them, because they were like sheep without a shepherd. So, he began teaching them many things.*

The disciples urged Jesus to send the crowd of 5,000 people away so they could go to town and buy something to eat—after all, they were in a deserted place with no food to feed such a great crowd. But Jesus said, *"You give them something to eat." They said to him, "That would take eight months of a man's wages! Are we to go and spend that much on bread and give it to them to eat?"*

*What?* The disciples were befuddled. The crowd was great; the resources, meager: five loaves of bread and two fish.

Jesus told the crowd to sit down on the grass in groups of hundreds and fifties. He took the five loaves and two fish, looked to heaven, blessed and broke the bread, and gave them to the disciples to set before the people. He divided the two fish among them. Everyone had enough to eat and there was plenty left over.

## DIALOGUE

1. *Jesus seems not to have anticipated that a quiet retreat with his disciples would turn into a response to the masses who invaded his privacy. What strikes you about this event?*

2. *Jesus saw something that moved him to respond to their need. What do you think it was?*

3. *Many have offered explanations for this miracle, and we can only imagine exactly how it happened. Perhaps more important than* how *it happened is* why *it happened. Why do you think this happened?*

4. *What lessons can you learn from Jesus' feeding of the 5,000?*

5. *What level of faith was reflected in the disciples' response to Jesus' instruction?*

6. *If you had been in their shoes, and had seen what they had seen with your own eyes, would you have had greater faith in Jesus' capacity to deliver what he offered? Why?*

7. *How can you relate this experience to your own life's journey?*

## JOURNAL

## CHAPTER FOUR

# BETHSAIDA, GENNESARET AND THE REGION OF TYRE AND SIDON

## *Segments 15-17*

### 15. How do you explain this relationship of the disciples to Jesus?

After feeding them, Jesus sent the crowd away and got back into the boat with the disciples and went to Bethsaida. Once there, he left his disciples and went alone into the hills to pray. By evening, the disciples had gone back out on the sea in their boat—perhaps to catch some fish. From the shore Jesus could see his disciples struggling to row against heavy winds. So he went to the disciples walking on the sea. The disciples were terrified. Jesus spoke to them saying, *"Take courage! It is I."*

He climbed into the boat with them and the wind died down. *They were completely amazed, for they had not understood about the loaves; their hearts were hardened.*

Jesus and his disciples arrived at a town called Gennesaret. *As soon as they had gotten out of the boat, people recognized Jesus. They ran throughout that whole region and carried the sick on mats to wherever they heard he was. ... They begged him to let them touch even the edge of his cloak, and all who touched him were healed.*

## DIALOGUE

1. *Given all that they had been through together, how would you describe the relationship between Jesus and his disciples at this point in their journey?*

2. *What do you think it means to have a "hardened heart"?*

3. *Given what they had experienced with Jesus, what can account for this* **hardening** *of the disciples' hearts?*

4. *How would you describe the present state of your heart—are you more or less receptive to Jesus?*

5. *If you chose to be more receptive to Jesus, what might you do?*

6. *If you became more receptive to Jesus, what difference do you think it would make in your life?*

7. *How can you relate this experience to your own life's journey?*

## JOURNAL

### 16. How would Jesus view our religious practices today?

Faithful Jews in Jesus' day observed the religious traditions taught by their religious leaders. For example, they would not eat without first washing their hands according to prescribed ritual; when they returned from the marketplace they would not eat before first purifying themselves; and they were nearly fanatical when it came to washing their cups and pots and pitchers of bronze.

Jesus' own disciples did not observe these traditions. So the scribes and Pharisees asked Jesus why his disciples didn't observe the traditions about eating food with unwashed hands. Jesus responded: *"Isaiah was right when he prophesied about you hypocrites; as it is written: 'These people honor me with their lips, but their hearts are far from me. They worship me in vain; their teachings are but rules taught by men.' You have let go of the commands of God and are holding on to the traditions of men."*

Jesus then gave an example of how one such tradition of men, which the scribes and Pharisees themselves advocated, corrupted the intent and spirit of the commandment to honor one's father and mother.

**GROUP DIALOGUE POWER TIP**

The safe and respectful dialogue environment creates "free space" for new thoughts to emerge. Spontaneity often births "revelations." When someone's contribution is not clear, it is often helpful to restate that person's contribution in different words and then ask the person if you "got it." Such attempts to clarify can surface new layers of thought that go beyond the initial contribution.

## DIALOGUE

1. *Based on this interchange between Jesus and the Pharisees, how do you think Jesus felt about religious traditions and observances? What was the main point he was making about them?*

2. *Can you identify any religious traditions and observances practiced today that Jesus might feel the same way about?*

3. *What underlying principle is Jesus affirming in this exchange?*

4. *Jesus called the Pharisees and scribes "hypocrites." What did he mean by that?*

5. *To what extent is your own faith guided more by religious traditions and observances than by the principles Jesus affirmed?*

6. *What difference would it make in your life if you put these principles first?*

7. *How can you relate this experience to your own life's journey?*

## JOURNAL

## 17. What was it about this Greek mother?

Jesus called the people and said to them, *"Nothing outside a man can make him unclean by going into him. Rather, it is what comes out of him that makes him unclean."* A little later, when they were in the house, the disciples asked Jesus what this meant. So he explained that the food we eat goes into the belly not into the heart! It is the misdeeds that come out of the heart that defile a person—because it reveals what is in the heart. Evil thoughts, sexual immorality, theft, murder, adultery, greed, malice, deceit, lewdness, envy, slander, arrogance, and folly come from the inside and make a person "unclean."

Jesus went to the region of Tyre and Sidon seeking some privacy in the home of a friend. But, again, privacy was elusive. A woman brought her little daughter to him and knelt at his feet and begged him to drive the demon out of the girl. The woman was Greek, born in the part of Syria known as Phoenicia—a Gentile. Jesus said to her: *"First, let the children eat all they want, for it is not right to take the children's bread and toss it to the dogs."* (Jesus apparently felt the focus of his ministry was on the Jews rather than on the Gentiles, such as the Greeks.) But the woman replied, *"Even the dogs under the table eat the children's crumbs." Jesus responded: "For such a reply you may go, the demon has left your daughter."*

### DIALOGUE

1. ***The scribes and Pharisees taught that certain "unclean" foods defile us as well as the dirt on our hands or eating utensils that are not ritually purified. What did Jesus mean when he used the term "unclean?"***

2. *When Jesus said that what comes out of us makes us unclean, what did he mean? Do you get his meaning?*

3. *Can you think of any questions you would like to ask Jesus about this concept of uncleanness coming from the heart?*

4. *What strikes you most about Jesus' response to the Greek woman's request to heal her daughter?*

5. *Jesus told the Greek mother that her daughter was healed based on her statement that even the dogs get the crumbs that fall from the children's table? What impressed Jesus about her statement? What was it about this mother that got Jesus' healing response?*

6. *Have you ever expressed faith as boldly as this Greek mother did?*

7. *How can you relate this experience to your own life's journey?*

### GROUP DIALOGUE POWER TIP

Although reaching agreement is not the goal of dialogue and suspending judgment about others' views and opinions is important, disagreements should be shared openly. When disagreements are shared, it is important to validate them as a different way of looking at a subject rather than trying to strong-arm an agreement. Disagreements can energize a group to seek meaning and clarity that goes beyond the initial conflicting views.

## JOURNAL

## CHAPTER FIVE

# THE REGION/VILLAGES OF DECAPOLIS AND CAESAREA PHILIPPI

## *Segments 18-20*

### 18. Has Jesus astonished you beyond measure?

Jesus returned to the Sea of Galilee through the region of Decapolis ("Ten Cities"). Some people brought a man who was deaf and could hardly talk to Jesus and begged him to lay hands upon the man and heal him. Jesus took the man aside and ministered to him with the touch of his hand and a few caring words: the man's ears were opened, his tongue was released, and he spoke plainly. *People were overwhelmed with amazement.*

#### DIALOGUE

1. ***Jesus healed this man who was deaf and suffered from a profound speech impediment. Do you think that any other part of the man was healed as a result? If so, what?***

2. ***Do you suspect that the people were overwhelmed with amazement only because of Jesus' healings?***

3. ***Could there have been something else that was amazing them? If so, what?***

4. *Mark tells us that the people were "overwhelmed with amazement." Have you ever witnessed an event, or been part of an experience, so profound that you would describe your reaction as "overwhelmed with amazement"? If so, what was it that so moved you?*

5. *Has Jesus done anything for you that overwhelmed you with amazement? If so, what? If so, how did that experience change you?*

6. *Do you find anything amazing about what Jesus represented?*

7. *How can you relate this experience to your own life's journey?*

## JOURNAL

## 19. How do you explain their lack of understanding?

The Pharisees came to Jesus and asked him to provide them with a miraculous sign from heaven. They were testing him. He denied their request, saying that no sign would be given to that generation. Jesus and his disciples then got into the boat and headed for the other side of the sea. Still pondering the Pharisees' request, Jesus told the disciples to watch out for the leaven of the Pharisees and of Herod. The disciples had not brought along much food and thought Jesus was talking about their lack of bread. Jesus reminded them of the feeding of the 5,000 and added: *"Why are you talking about having no bread? Do you still not see or understand? Are your hearts hardened? Do you have eyes but fail to see, and ears but fail to hear?"*

Jesus and the disciples moved on through the villages around Caesarea Philippi at the southern base of Mount Hermon. On the way Jesus asked his disciples, *"Who do people say I am?"* They told him that some thought he was John the baptizer raised from the dead, some others thought he was the prophet Elijah, and still others thought he was one of the other prophets. Jesus then challenged them: *"But what about you? Who do you say I am?"* Peter answered, *"You are the Christ."*

When Peter spoke up and said, *"You are the Christ"* ("the Anointed One" in Greek), it is likely he sensed that Jesus was the Messiah, the King through whom the people of God would experience God's ultimate victory in history.

Jesus warned the disciples to keep this to themselves.

## DIALOGUE

1. ***Leaven is a potent ingredient that causes dough to rise. When Jesus warned the disciples about the leaven of the Pharisees and of Herod, what do you think he was referring to?***

2. ***What do you make of the disciples' lack of understanding? What do you make of Jesus' frustration with their lack of understanding?***

3. ***Peter's response to Jesus' question about his identity was, "You are the Christ!" If you said that "Jesus is the Christ" what would you mean by it?***

4. ***Would you be hesitant to make such a statement? If so, why?***

5. ***Why do you suppose Jesus charged his disciples to keep his identity secret?***

6. ***Can you think of anything about Jesus that he might not want his followers to tell about him today? If so, what would that be?***

7. ***How can you relate this experience to your own life's journey?***

**JOURNAL**

## 20. Are you ready to deny yourself?

After urging the disciples to keep his identity to themselves, Jesus told them what lay ahead: He would be rejected by the elders, the chief priests, and the teachers of the law and ultimately be killed and after three days rise again. Peter, outraged at the very suggestion of such an end of Jesus' ministry, took Jesus aside and rebuked him for saying such things. But Jesus rebuked Peter. *"Get behind me, Satan!"* he said. *"You do not have in mind the things of God, but the things of men."*

Jesus called together his disciples and the multitude to hear what he had to say next.

*"If anyone would come after me, he must deny himself and take up his cross and follow me. For whoever wants to save his life will lose it, but whoever loses his life for me and for the gospel will save it. What good is it for a man to gain the whole world, yet forfeit his soul?"*

**GROUP DIALOGUE POWER TIP**

It is important to assume that members of the group have pieces of the answers to the questions raised in the dialogue and that together the group can craft a new and better answer. Celebrate new insights, greater clarity, and deeper understandings when they occur. In disclosing such shifts in their thinking, group members demonstrate an openness that can be contagious.

## DIALOGUE

1. ***When Jesus told the disciples what lay ahead, Peter couldn't believe what he was hearing and rebuked Jesus. Jesus, in turn, rebuked Peter in the strongest language possible. (A) If you were in Peter's shoes, how would you feel about this? (B) If you were in Jesus' shoes, what feelings would you have?***

2. *What would it mean for you to* **deny yourself?**

3. *What would it mean for you to* **take up your cross?**

4. *What would it mean for you to* **lose your life** *for Jesus' sake?*

5. *What did Jesus mean by "for the sake of the gospel?"*

6. *What do you think Jesus meant when he asked what good it was to gain the world but forfeit one's soul?*

7. *How can you relate this experience to your own life's journey?*

## JOURNAL

## CHAPTER SIX

# THE MOUNT OF TRANSFIGURATION

## *Segments 21-24*

### 21. What did Jesus mean by "the Kingdom of God"?

Jesus had more to say on this occasion. *"If anyone is ashamed of me and my words in this adulterous and sinful generation, the Son of Man will be ashamed of him when he comes in his Father's glory with the holy angels."* Jesus concluded his remarks with the statement that the Kingdom of God would come with power within the lifetime of some of those present.

Mary Ely Lyman said: "In Jesus' thought the Kingdom meant the righteous rule of God. ... In so far as men accept the will of God and live by it, the Kingdom is a present reality; in so far as they reject it, the Kingdom is thought of as in the future. This paradox of the present and of the future is shown in Jesus' prayer: *'Thine is the Kingdom. Thy Kingdom come.'* ... He (Jesus) commended no theoretical position about the organization of society ... but assumed that, as men accept the rule of God and live under it, they become a spiritual community in which justice and neighborliness and mutual honor and concern for each other as children of God will prevail." [9]

## DIALOGUE

1. *Based on what you now know about Jesus, under what circumstances might you be ashamed of him?*

2. *Can you imagine any circumstances in which Jesus might be ashamed of you? If so, what would they be?*

3. *Based on what you know about Jesus, what is your understanding of the* **Kingdom of God***?*

4. *What do you make of the paradox of the present and the future to which Mary Ely Lyman referred?*

5. *As you look around you at our world, do you see any evidence that we live in the Kingdom of God? If you were called into court as a witness and asked to provide evidence for the Kingdom of God on earth, what evidence would you offer?*

6. *Are there any questions you would like to ask Jesus about this Kingdom? If so, what?*

7. *How can you relate this experience to your own life's journey?*

## JOURNAL

## 22. What does this tell you about Peter?

Jesus took Peter, James, and John and led them high up on a mountain—most likely Mount Hermon whose snow-capped peaks rise over 9,000 feet. It is a four-hour walk from Caesarea Philippi to the base of the mountain, and it takes about seven hours to climb to the summit. *There he was transfigured before them. His clothes became dazzling white, whiter than anyone in the world could bleach them. And there appeared before them Elijah and Moses, who were talking to Jesus.*

*Peter said to Jesus, "Rabbi, it is good for us to be here. Let us put up three shelters—one for you, one for Moses and one for Elijah." (He did not know what to say, they were so frightened.)*

The shelters Peter had in mind had several meanings to Jews. (In *Old Testament* days, booths were temporary shelters from which to watch and protect crops ready for harvesting. In association with the Feast of the Tabernacle, which marked the completion of the harvest and commemorated the wanderings of the Hebrews in the wilderness, Peter may have thought of booths as temporary shelters for use until the messianic era arrived.) A cloud enveloped Jesus and the three disciples and they heard a voice saying: *"This is my Son, whom I love. Listen to him!"* Then when they looked around they saw no one with them but Jesus.

Elijah and Moses lived and died hundreds of years before this time. Since Peter was likely the primary source for Mark's gospel, this is an eyewitness account.

### DIALOGUE

1. ***In the Transfiguration, why do you think Elijah and Moses were there in dialogue with Jesus?***

2. *What is the implication of the Transfiguration for those who die (that is: all of us)?*

3. *If you had been there, would you have been "frightened"? Why or why not?*

4. *What does Peter's proposal—to build memorial shelters—tell you about Peter?*

5. *Do you believe this really happened? If not, why not? If so, what does it mean?*

6. *Jesus said that his followers hear his voice. To what extent are you able to hear Jesus?*

7. *How can you relate this experience to your own life's journey?*

## JOURNAL

**23. How does Elijah fit in with Jesus?**

*As they were coming down the mountain, Jesus gave them orders not to tell anyone what they had seen until the Son of Man had risen from the dead.* They did as Jesus asked but were curious and asked: *"Why do the teachers of the law say that Elijah must come first?" Jesus replied, "To be sure, Elijah does come first, and restores all things ... But I tell you, Elijah has come, and they have done to him everything they wished, just as it is written about him."*

(Jesus always used the term "Son of Man" in reference to himself; it occurs 81 times in the Gospels. Variations of the term are found in the *Old Testament,* and it may have been a messianic title.)

*Who was Elijah?* Elijah (whose Hebrew name means, "My God is Yahweh") was one of the greatest of the prophets. He lived some 800 years before Jesus, and the account of his life is recorded in the Bible books 1 and 2 Kings. The highlights of his illustrious life include raising the dead, calling down fire from the sky, and bypassing death by being caught up to heaven in a whirlwind.

**DIALOGUE**

1. ***When Jesus said "Elijah has come," who do you think he was referring to?***

2. ***Why do you think Jesus associated himself and his ministry as the Son of Man with the prophets and their prophecies?***

3. ***Why do you think Jesus instructed Peter, James, and John not to tell anyone what they had seen until the Son of Man had risen from the dead?***

4. *There was a period of 400 years between the last prophet of the Hebrew Bible (what we call the Old Testament) and the birth of Jesus. What do you think accounts for this gap—400 years of silence?*

5. *Take some time to explore your view of God. How does your view of God make a difference in your life? If you had a different view of God, how would your life be different?*

6. *Was there a time in your life when you had a different view of God? If so, what difference (if any) did it make.*

7. *How can you relate this experience to your own life's journey?*

**JOURNAL**

## 24. What help do you need for your unbelief?

When Jesus, Peter, James, and John came down from the mountain they found the other disciples in the midst of a great crowd. The scribes (teachers of the Law) were arguing with the disciples. The crowd ran out to greet Jesus and before the disciples got a chance to tell Jesus what they were arguing about with the scribes, a man brought his epileptic son to Jesus. He had asked the disciples to heal him, but they were not able. The father pleaded: *"But if you can do anything, take pity on us and help us." "'If you can'?" said Jesus. "Everything is possible for him who believes." Immediately the boy's father exclaimed, "I do believe, help me overcome my unbelief!"* Jesus cured the child of his epilepsy.

## DIALOGUE

1. ***What do you believe contributed to the healing of this epileptic boy? What made it possible?***

2. ***Why do you suppose the disciples were unable to heal the boy?***

3. ***What do you think Jesus meant when he responded to the man: "'If you can'?"***

4. ***The boy's father was honest enough to confess that he struggled: "I do believe, help me overcome my unbelief." What does Jesus' healing tell us about how he deals with this tension between belief and unbelief?***

5. ***Have you ever felt this tension between belief and unbelief? If so, how does Jesus deal with* your *tension between belief and unbelief?***

6. ***What help do you need to overcome your unbelief?***

7. ***How can you relate this experience to your own life's journey?***

## JOURNAL

## CHAPTER SEVEN

# GALILEE

## *Segments 25-26*

### 25. What don't you understand about Jesus?

Jesus tried to keep a low profile as he journeyed through Galilee so that he would have enough time to teach his disciples more about what was ahead. *"The Son of man is going to be betrayed into the hands of men. They will kill him, and after three days he will rise." But they did not understand what he meant and were afraid to ask him about it.*

As they were walking to Capernaum, the disciples (supposing they were out of Jesus' earshot) discussed which one of them was the greatest. Jesus knew what they were discussing and said to them, *"If anyone wants to be first, he must be the very last, and the servant of all." He took a little child, and had him stand among them. Taking him in his arms, he said to them, "Whoever welcomes one of these little children in my name welcomes me; and whoever welcomes me does not welcome me but the one who sent me."*

Jesus knew that the religious leaders did not understand him and he anticipated being arrested and killed. Then he told his chosen disciples that they must be servants of all.

## DIALOGUE

1. *Does it seem strange to you that given all that they had seen with their own eyes and heard with their own ears, the disciples not only didn't understand Jesus but were afraid to ask for clarification?*

2. *Are there some things that you don't you understand about Jesus? Is so, what?*

3. *If you were given a chance to have a heart-to-heart talk with Jesus right now, what would you say to him about what you need to understand?*

4. *If you had been there among the disciples when they were discussing who was the greatest, what would you have said to them?*

5. *Jesus held the child before his disciples as a model of himself—welcoming a child is welcoming God. What is it about a child that puts ego in proper perspective?*

6. *If you had been one of the Twelve, at this point in the ministry of Jesus would you continue to be a follower? Why or why not?*

7. *How can you relate this experience to your own life's journey?*

## JOURNAL

## 26. Have you received the Kingdom of God like a child?

Mark reports a list of acts that would lead to grave consequences.

- Whoever leads a child who believes in Jesus to sin ... it would be better to have a great millstone hung round his neck and be thrown into the sea.

- If your hand causes you to sin, cut if off... it is better to be maimed than with two hands to go to the unquenchable fire of hell.

- If your foot causes you to sin, cut it off... it is better to enter life lame than with two feet to be thrown into hell.

- If your eye causes you to sin, pluck it out ... it is better to enter the Kingdom of God with one eye than with two eyes to be thrown into hell.

As Jesus was in a spirited discussion with the Pharisees, some people brought children to Jesus so he could touch them. The disciples intervened and scolded them—perhaps not wanting them to disturb his teaching. When Jesus saw what they were doing, he was indignant and said to them, *"Let the children come to me, and do not hinder them, for the kingdom of God belongs to such as these. I tell you the truth, anyone who will not receive the kingdom of God like a little child will never enter it." And he took the children in his arms, put his hands on them and blessed them.*

## DIALOGUE

**Jesus painted vivid pictures of the consequences of yielding to temptations.**

1. ***What do these words mean to you? What does it mean to you when you hear Jesus say that it is better to cut off your hand than to risk hell?***

2. ***If you struggle with any of those behaviors that Jesus mentioned, have you done anything to correct them? If not, what could you do to deal with them?***

3. ***What are you willing to do to correct those behaviors not yet corrected?***

### GROUP DIALOGUE POWER TIP

Marcia Emery identified five sources of intuitive discovery: clues from everyday experiences, clues from sensations such as a "gut feeling," feelings such as immediate like or dislike, a sudden flash of understanding, and an awareness of or connection with something greater than the physical world.

4. *What does Jesus mean by receiving the Kingdom of God like a child?*

5. *What are some things about a child that Jesus might have had in mind?*

6. *How can an adult receive the Kingdom of God like a little child? Have you done so?*

7. *How can you relate this experience to your own life's journey?*

## JOURNAL

**CHAPTER EIGHT**

# THE REGION OF JUDEA

## *Segments 27-30*

### 27. How did Jesus view marriage and divorce?

Jesus and his disciples went to the region of Judea beyond the Jordan River. Crowds continued to gather and Jesus continued to teach them. As usual, there were critics and skeptics in the crowd. Some Pharisees put Jesus to the test with a question about whether it was lawful for a man to divorce his wife. *"What did Moses command you?" he replied. They said, "Moses permitted a man to write a certificate of divorce and send her away." "It was because your hearts were hard that Moses wrote you this law," Jesus replied. "But at the beginning of creation God made them male and female. For this reason a man will leave his father and mother and be united to his wife and the two will become one flesh. So they are no longer two, but one. Therefore what God has joined together, let man not separate."* When the disciples asked Jesus to elaborate on this, he said that anyone who divorces and remarries commits adultery.

**DIALOGUE**

1. ***Jesus made his position clear on marriage and divorce. Is there anything you would like to ask him about this?***

2. ***Given everything you know about Jesus, how do you think he would respond to your questions?***

3. *Jesus described the marriage of man and woman as a fusion of flesh in which two become one. What kind of love does this imply?*

4. *How would you define the love required for a Christian marriage?*

5. *To what extent are you able to express that kind of love?*

6. *How do you think Jesus would respond to a divorced person who came to him? To a divorced person who was remarried? To a person who was divorced and remarried more than once?*

7. *How can you relate this experience to your own life's journey?*

## GROUP DIALOGUE POWER TIP

Barriers to effective group interaction:

- Ingrained habits of non-listening
- Pride that gets in the way
- Resistance to change
- Different personalities and personality types

## JOURNAL

## 28. What did Jesus say about how we enter the Kingdom of God?

A man came to Jesus and asked what he must do to inherit eternal life. Jesus reminded him of the Ten Commandments. The man responded that he had kept them since he was a boy. *Jesus looked at him and loved him. "One thing you lack," he said, "Go, and sell everything you have and give to the poor, and you will have treasure in heaven. Then come, follow me." At this the man's face fell. He went away sad, because he had great wealth.*

Jesus then said to his disciples: *"How hard it is for the rich to enter the kingdom of God!"* These words amazed the disciples. But Jesus added this: *"It is easier for a camel to go through the eye of a needle than for a rich man to enter the kingdom of God."* The disciples were even more amazed and asked: *"Then who can be saved?" Jesus looked at them and said, "With man this is impossible, but not with God, all things are possible with God."*

# JESUS AND THE RICH YOUNG RULER

## DIALOGUE

1. *What is the underlying message of Jesus to the man with great possessions?*

2. *Do you think this means that those who are wealthy cannot be saved?*

3. *What would it have taken for the wealthy man to follow Jesus?*

4. *What difference did his obedience to the commandments make in his life? What difference does your obedience to them make in your life?*

5. *What does Jesus mean by "with God all things are possible"?*

6. *What is Jesus saying about how we enter the kingdom of God?*

7. *How can you relate this experience to your own life's journey?*

## JOURNAL

## 29. Are you able to be great by being a servant?

James and John, the sons of Zebedee, asked Jesus: *"We want you to do for us whatever we ask." "What do you want me to do for you?" he asked. They replied, "Let one of us sit at your right and the other at your left in your glory." "You don't know what you are asking," Jesus said. "Can you drink the cup I drink or be baptized with the baptized with the baptism I am baptized with?" "We can," they answered.*

Jesus told the brothers that it was not his to assign seating in the Kingdom. When the other disciples heard this, they were angry at James and John. But again Jesus reminded them, *"Whoever wants to become great among you must be your servant and whoever wants to be first must be slave to all. For even the Son of man did not come to be served, but to serve, and to give his life as a ransom for many."*

### DIALOGUE

1. ***What is your view about "status" in God's Kingdom? How does it square with the ideals of our culture? What is the role of competition in a "last shall be first, least shall be greatest" society?***

2. ***In what ways was Jesus a servant leader? Did he practice what he preached when it came to servant leadership? If so, in what ways?***

3. ***Is servant leadership important for a moral society? If so, in what ways?***

4. ***To what extent are you a servant leader as Jesus described it?***

5. ***What would it take to make you more effective in your servant leadership?***

6. *What do you think the results would be if you were more effective in your servant leadership?*

7. *How can you relate this experience to your own life's journey?*

### JOURNAL

## 30. What do you want Jesus to do for you?

Jesus and his disciples came to Jericho where Bartimaeus, a blind beggar, cried out, *"Jesus, Son of David, have mercy on me!"* Those nearby rebuked him and told him to be silent, but he cried out all the more. Jesus stopped and called for the man. The man sprang up and went to Jesus. *"What do you want me to do for you?"* Jesus asked. *The blind man said, "Rabbi, I want to see." "Go," said Jesus, "your faith has healed you." Immediately he received his sight and followed Jesus along the road.*

### DIALOGUE

1. *How does blind Bartimaeus express his faith?*

2. *If Jesus were here right now and asked you,* "What do you want me to do for you?" *how would you respond?*

3. *Does it surprise you that religious leaders and the disciples were reserved and skeptical about trusting Jesus when ordinary people with extraordinary needs were ready to trust him and put their faith in him to meet their needs? If so, why?*

4. *As you reflect on your journey with Jesus, how would you define "faith"?*

5. *How would you describe your faith? Do you think there is any difference between belief and faith? Why or why not?*

6. *In many cases Jesus seemed more ready to accept those who listened to him than they were to accept that he accepted them. What do you make of this?*

7. *How can you relate this experience to your own life's journey?*

## JOURNAL

## GROUP DIALOGUE POWER TIP

Barriers to effective group interaction:

- Disrespect for one another may suppress openness
- Lack of trust—resistance to reveal "secrets"
- Egos—would require increased vulnerability
- Competitiveness including jockeying for influence

Segments 1–30 of this book describe the ministry of Jesus reported in Chapters 1–10 of *The Gospel of Mark*. Segments 31–52 describe Jesus' experiences and his initiatives to reveal God's incredible love for men and women and the sacrifice involved in our redemption and renewal.

The four maps that follow were provided by Zondervan.

## THE ROMAN EMPIRE

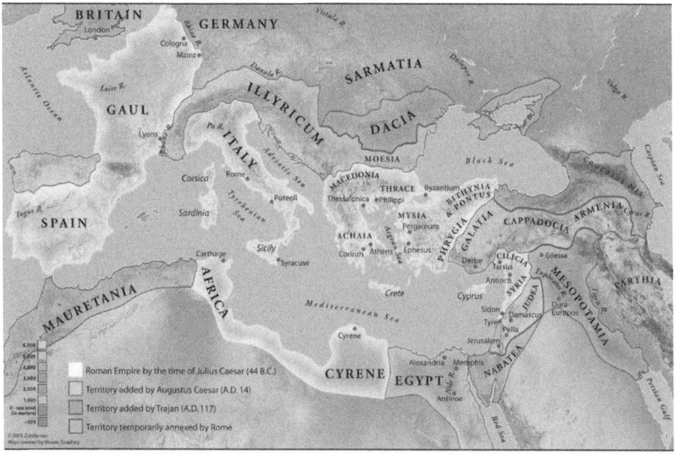

## THE HOLY LAND AND SINAI

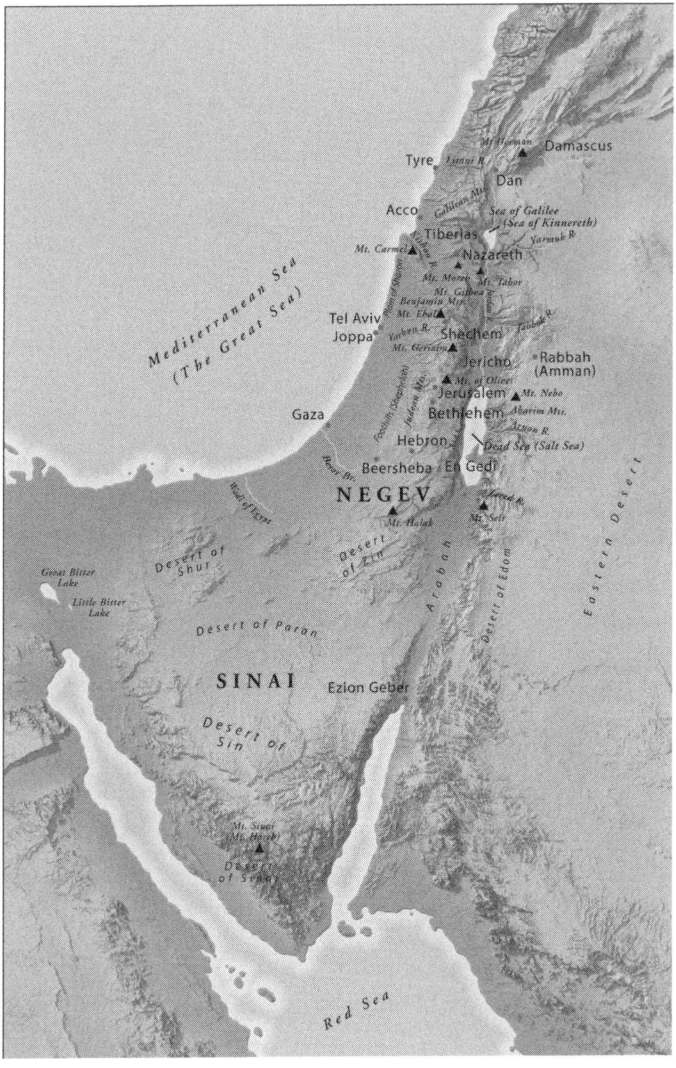
Mt. Hermon
Damascus
Tyre
Litani R.
Dan
Galilean Mts.
Acco
Sea of Galilee
(Sea of Kinnereth)
Tiberias
Yarmuk R.
Mt. Carmel
Kishon R.
Nazareth
Mt. Moreh
Mt. Tabor
Mt. Gilboa
Benjamin Mts.
Mediterranean Sea
(The Great Sea)
Plain of Sharon
Tel Aviv
Mt. Ebal
Joppa
Yarkon R.
Shechem
Jabbok R.
Mt. Gerizim
Jericho
Rabbah
(Amman)
Foothills (Shephelah)
Judean Mts.
Mt. of Olives
Jerusalem
Mt. Nebo
Gaza
Bethlehem
Abarim Mts.
Arnon R.
Hebron
Dead Sea (Salt Sea)
Besor Br.
Beersheba
En Gedi
NEGEV
Wadi of Egypt
Zered R.
Mt. Halak
Mt. Seir
Desert of Zin
Desert of Shur
Arabah
Desert of Edom
Eastern Desert
Great Bitter Lake
Little Bitter Lake
Desert of Paran
SINAI
Ezion Geber
Desert of Sin
Mt. Sinai
(Mt. Horeb)
Desert of Sinai
Red Sea

# THE HOLY LAND IN THE TIME OF JESUS

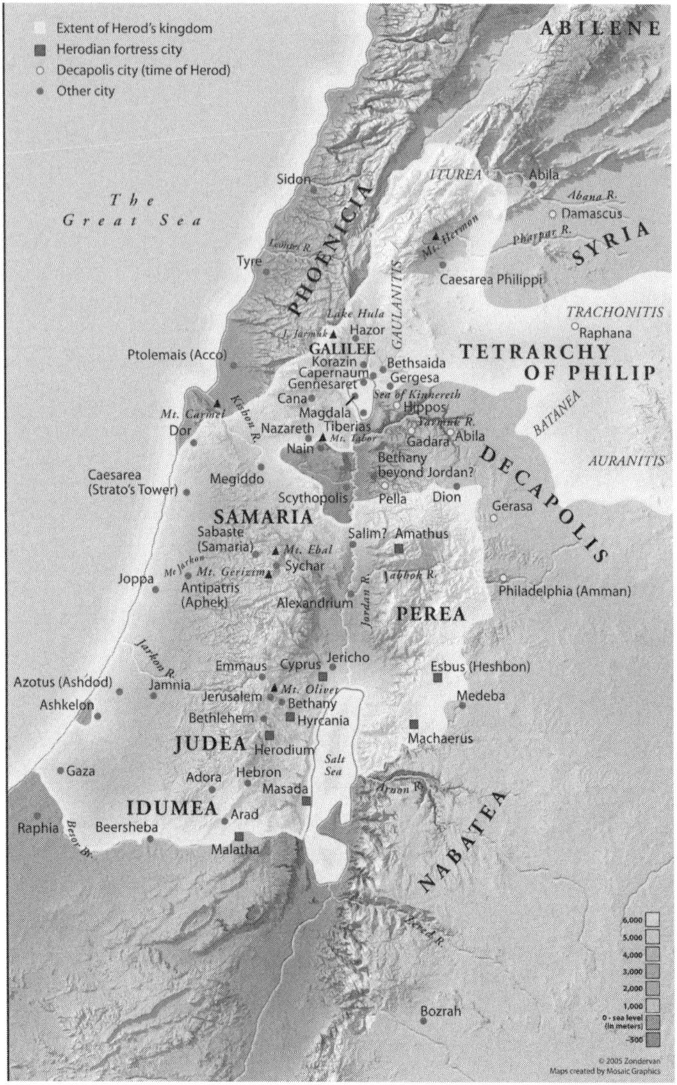
Extent of Herod's kingdom
Herodian fortress city
Decapolis city (time of Herod)
Other city
ABILENE
ITUREA
Abila
Abana R.
Damascus
Pharpar R.
SYRIA
Sidon
The Great Sea
PHOENICIA
Mt. Hermon
Tyre
GAULANITIS
Caesarea Philippi
TRACHONITIS
Raphana
Lake Hula
Hazor
GALILEE
TETRARCHY OF PHILIP
Ptolemais (Acco)
Korazin
Bethsaida
Capernaum
Gergesa
Gennesaret
Sea of Kinnereth
Cana
Hippos
Mt. Carmel
Kishon R.
Magdala
Yarmuk R.
BATANEA
Dor
Nazareth
Tiberias
Abila
Mt. Tabor
Gadara
Nain
DECAPOLIS
Bethany beyond Jordan?
AURANITIS
Caesarea (Strato's Tower)
Megiddo
Scythopolis
Pella
Dion
Gerasa
SAMARIA
Sabaste (Samaria)
Salim?
Amathus
Mt. Ebal
Sychar
Mt. Gerizim
Jabbok R.
Joppa
Antipatris (Aphek)
Jordan R.
Philadelphia (Amman)
Alexandrium
PEREA
Jarkon R.
Emmaus
Cyprus
Jericho
Esbus (Heshbon)
Azotus (Ashdod)
Jamnia
Mt. Olivet
Jerusalem
Bethany
Medeba
Ashkelon
Bethlehem
Hyrcania
Machaerus
JUDEA
Herodium
Salt Sea
Gaza
Adora
Hebron
Masada
Arnon R.
IDUMEA
Arad
Raphia
Besor Br.
Beersheba
Malatha
NABATEA
Zered R.
Bozrah
6,000
5,000
4,000
3,000
2,000
1,000
0 - sea level (in meters)
-500
© 2005 Zondervan
Maps created by Mosaic Graphics

# JERUSALEM IN THE TIME OF JESUS

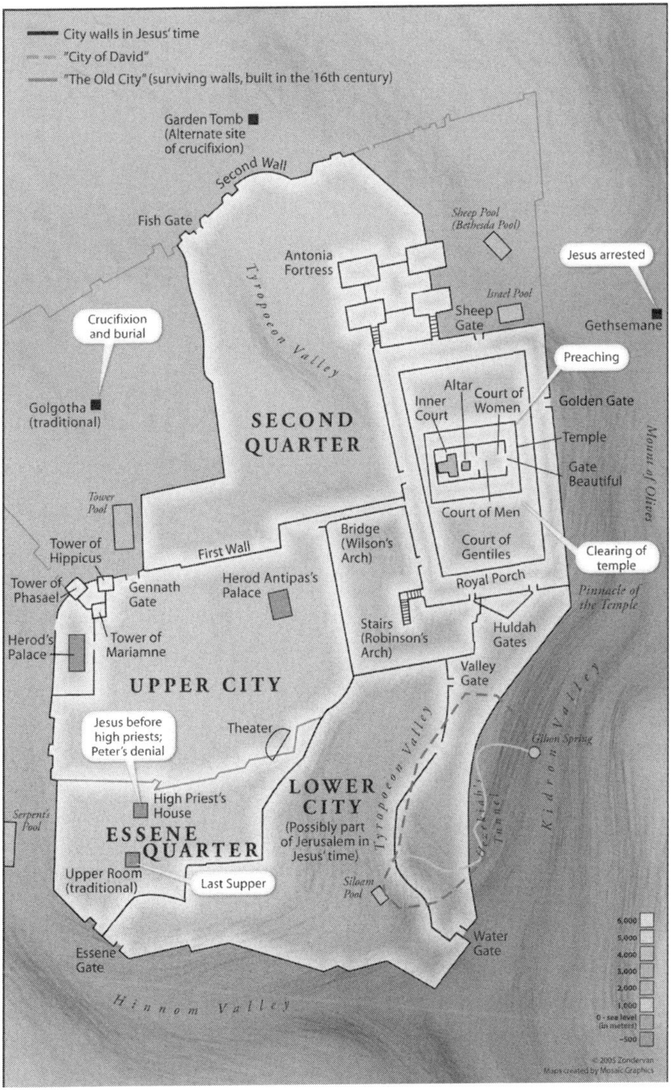
City walls in Jesus' time
"City of David"
"The Old City" (surviving walls, built in the 16th century)
Garden Tomb (Alternate site of crucifixion)
Second Wall
Fish Gate
Antonia Fortress
Tyropoeon Valley
Sheep Pool (Bethesda Pool)
Jesus arrested
Gethsemane
Israel Pool
Sheep Gate
Crucifixion and burial
Golgotha (traditional)
Preaching
Altar
Inner Court
Court of Women
Golden Gate
SECOND QUARTER
Temple
Mount of Olives
Gate Beautiful
Tower Pool
Court of Men
Tower of Hippicus
First Wall
Bridge (Wilson's Arch)
Court of Gentiles
Clearing of temple
Tower of Phasael
Gennath Gate
Herod Antipas's Palace
Royal Porch
Pinnacle of the Temple
Herod's Palace
Tower of Mariamne
Stairs (Robinson's Arch)
Huldah Gates
Valley Gate
UPPER CITY
Jesus before high priests; Peter's denial
Theater
Gihon Spring
Kidron Valley
LOWER CITY
High Priest's House
Serpent's Pool
ESSENE QUARTER
(Possibly part of Jerusalem in Jesus' time)
Tyropoeon Valley
Hezekiah's Tunnel
Upper Room (traditional)
Last Supper
Siloam Pool
Water Gate
Essene Gate
Hinnom Valley
6,000
5,000
4,000
3,000
2,000
1,000
0 - sea level (in meters)
-500
© 2005 Zondervan
Maps created by Mosaic Graphics

## CHAPTER NINE

# BETHPHAGE AND BETHANY AT THE MOUNT OF OLIVES

## *Segment 31*

**31. How do you explain this approach to a triumphal entry?**

Jesus and the disciples approached Jerusalem and came to Bethphage and Bethany at the Mount of Olives (a hilltop about 2,600 feet above the Mediterranean Sea located on the eastern outskirts of Jerusalem). Jesus sent two of his disciples out with the charge: *"Go to the village ahead of you, and just as you enter it, you will find a colt tied there, which no one has ever ridden. Untie it and bring it here. If any one asks you, 'Why are you doing this?' tell him, 'The Lord needs it and will send it back shortly.'"*

They did as they were told and got the response Jesus predicted. *When they brought the colt to Jesus and threw their cloaks over it, he sat on it. Many people spread their cloaks on the road, while others spread branches they had cut in the fields. Those who went ahead and those who followed shouted, "Hosanna! Blessed is he who comes in the name of the Lord! Blessed is the coming kingdom of our father David!"*

### DIALOGUE

**This episode is how the day Christians call Palm Sunday began.**

## ENTRY OF JESUS INTO JERUSALEM

1. *In that day Roman soldiers and foreign dignitaries made dramatic entries into Jerusalem with all the fanfare of royalty. Does this ride on colt-back seem to you to be the kind of entry appropriate for someone inviting citizenship in the Kingdom of God? Why or why not?*

2. *If you had been in the crowd, how might you have reacted? Why?*

3. *How would you describe the Jesus of this "triumphal entry"?*

4. *Would your impression of Jesus on Palm Sunday have inspired you to be more or less open and receptive to him during the week that followed? Why or why not?*

5. *If you were a reporter for the* **Jerusalem Gazette** *covering this event, what would you likely report? What would your lead for the story have been?*

6. *If you had been able to interview Jesus during the course of this entry what do you think he would have disclosed to you about this day? Are there certain questions you would have asked him about it?*

7. *How can you relate this experience to your own life's journey?*

## JOURNAL

## CHAPTER TEN

# JERUSALEM AND BETHANY

## *Segments 32-37*

### 32. What would a house of prayer for all nations be like?

Jesus and the disciples entered Jerusalem and went to the Temple to look around for a while before returning to Bethany. The next day, on their way back to Jerusalem, Jesus was hungry so he approached a leafy fig tree but found nothing but leaves because it was not the season for figs. *Then he said to the tree, "May no one ever eat fruit from you again."*

They arrived in Jerusalem and entered the Temple. Jerusalem at the time of the Passover Festival was the center of the spiritual universe for the Jews. Hundreds of thousands of pilgrims came to celebrate the holiday. All male Israelites were required to pay the Temple tax with special coins (two drachmas). People who came from far-off lands needed to have their native currency converted into the required currency. Those who converted the currency were called "moneychangers," and some levied a hefty surcharge for the service.

The Temple trade was a "racket" of sorts controlled by the party known as the Sadducees (the priestly class in Israel). In addition to paying the Temple tax, those who came to worship at the Temple were required to purchase sacrificial animals from the Temple merchants who sold wine and sacrificial animals at a steep margin.

On entering the Temple, Jesus overturned the moneychangers' tables and the seats of those selling pigeons and stopped those carrying things through the Temple and said: *"Is it not written, 'My house will be called a house of prayer for all nations?' But you have made it a den of robbers."* When the chief priests and scribes heard this, they began plotting to destroy Jesus. They feared him because the multitude was astonished at his teaching and, what was worse, he was "profaning" the Temple and its worship. (Priests ministered in the temple. The Chief Priest presided over the Sanhedrin, the high court for religious matters.)

## DIALOGUE

1. ***What strikes you most about this visit to the Temple?***

2. ***Can you sense the tension between Jesus and the "religious establishment" mounting? Can you empathize with the disciples and what they must have been feeling and sensing? If so, how does that feel?***

3. ***Who is Jesus confronting in this segment? Why? Do you think this confrontation squares with what most people think about Jesus?***

4. ***To what extent do you think the religious leaders in charge of the Temple were sincere in their management of the Temple?***

5. ***Do you see examples today of religious leaders appearing to manage religious institutions in ways that would be offensive to Jesus? How?***

6. *If you saw some religious leaders taking advantage of people seeking God would you be willing to stand up against the religious leaders? Why?*

7. *How can you relate this experience to your own life's journey?*

## JOURNAL

### 33. By what authority did Jesus do these things?

On their way back to Jerusalem the next morning, they saw the fig tree withered away to its roots. Peter called Jesus' attention to it and Jesus answered: *"Have faith in God. I tell you the truth, if anyone says to this mountain, 'Go throw yourself into the sea,' and does not doubt in his heart, but believes that what he says will happen—it will be done for him. Therefore, I tell you, whatever you ask for in prayer, believe that you have received it, and it will be yours."*

When they got back to the Temple in Jerusalem, the chief priests, scribes, and elders questioned Jesus about the source of authority for his actions. *Jesus replied, "I will ask you one question. Answer me, and I will tell you by what authority I am doing these things. John's baptism—was it from heaven, or from men? Tell me." They discussed it among themselves and said, "If we say, 'From heaven,' he will ask, 'Why didn't you believe him?' But if we say, 'From men'…" (They feared the people, for everyone held that John was a prophet.) So they answered Jesus, "We don't know." Jesus said, "Neither will I tell you by what authority I am doing these things."*

## DIALOGUE

1. *Do you think Jesus intended us to take his words about prayer literally?*

2. *What do you think Jesus was conveying about the relationship between prayer and faith?*

3. *To what extent do you have the kind of faith "that can move mountains"? Have you ever had a "mountain-moving" answer to prayer? If so, what was it?*

4. *Why do you suppose Jesus was not more willing to disclose the source of his authority to the religious leaders?*

5. *If you had witnessed Jesus' cleansing of the Temple and heard his teachings, as we have in our group reading and dialogue, what evidence could you present for the authority of Jesus?*

6. *On the basis of that evidence, would you trust his leadership?*

7. *How can you relate this experience to your own life's journey?*

## JOURNAL

**34. What does this parable mean to you?**

While still in the Temple with the chief priests, scribes, and elders, Jesus spoke to them in parables. "*A man planted a vineyard. He put a wall around it, dug a pit for the wine press and built a watchtower. Then he rented the vineyard to some farmers and went away on a journey. At harvest time he sent a servant to the tenants to collect from them some of the fruit of the vineyard. But they seized him, beat him and sent him away empty-handed. Then he sent another servant to them; they struck this man on the head and treated him shamefully. He sent still another and that one they killed. He sent many others; some of them they beat others they killed.*

*"He had one left to send, a son, whom he loved. He sent him last of all, saying, 'They will respect my son.' But the tenants said to one another, 'This is the heir. Come, let us kill him, and the inheritance will be ours.' So they took him and killed him, and threw him out of the vineyard."*

The Temple leaders knew he spoke the parable against them and wondered how they might secure Jesus' arrest. But they were afraid of the crowd, so they left him and went away.

### DIALOGUE

1. ***Do you think it likely that anyone missed the point of this parable? If so, who and why?***

2. ***What does the parable say about the man who planted the vineyard and went away?***

3. ***Who might the servants in this parable represent?***

4. ***What does the parable say about those who rejected the son?***

5. ***Do you find it hard to believe the behavior of those who rejected the son? Why?***

6. *What do you think Jesus meant by "at harvest time"?*

7. *How can you relate this experience to your own life's journey?*

**GROUP DIALOGUE POWER TIP**

Dialogue does not proceed stepwise like climbing a ladder. It is communication that stimulates the growth of people and groups when participants are free for open exchange and clarity. The deeper experience we have in dialogue, the greater potential we have for personal and group transformation.

## JOURNAL

## 35. Why were religious leaders so adamant in their conflict with Jesus?

The religious leaders sent Pharisees and Herodians to entrap Jesus. They put this question to him: *"Teacher, we know you are a man of integrity. You aren't swayed by men, because you pay no attention to who they are; but you teach the way of God in accordance with the truth. Is it right to pay taxes to Caesar or not? Should we pay or shouldn't we?" But Jesus knew their hypocrisy. "Why are you trying to trap me? Bring me a denarius and let me look at it." They brought the coin, and he asked them, "Whose portrait is this? And whose inscription?" "Caesar's," they replied. Then Jesus said to them, "Give to Caesar what is Caesar's and to God what is God's."*

In spite of his transparent parable and the apparent support of the multitude who believed that Jesus was indeed someone special and the fact that he was able to outsmart those who attempted to make him appear heretical, the religious leaders persisted in their efforts to destroy Jesus.

## DIALOGUE

1. ***Why were the religious leaders so adamant in their efforts to get rid of Jesus?***

2. ***If Jesus was a threat (as the religious leaders obviously believed he was), what was at risk? What was in jeopardy?***

3. ***Do you think Jesus still poses a threat to religious leaders and the "religious establishment" today? If so, in what ways?***

4. ***What things belong to God?***

5. ***What does it mean to give to God what is God's? What does it mean to give to Caesar what is Caesar's?***

6. ***Do you think God has a*** **standard** ***for our stewardship of those things that belong to him? If so, what do you think that standard is?***

7. ***How can you relate this experience to your own life's journey?***

## JOURNAL

## 36. Why does Jesus put up with the "games" of the religious leaders?

The chief priests, scribes, elders, and Pharisees had taken their shots at Jesus—confronting him about various matters (such as why his disciples ate with unwashed hands and why he "broke" the Sabbath by healing sick people on Saturdays). Then came the Sadducees, the priestly class, who did not believe in life after death (resurrection), and they challenged him with this hypothetical situation. *"Moses wrote for us that if a man's brother dies and leaves a wife but no children, the man must marry the widow and have children for his brother. Now there were seven brothers. The first one married and died without leaving any children. The second married the widow, but he also died, leaving no child. It was the same with the third. In fact, none of the seven left any children. Last of all, the woman died too. At the resurrection whose wife will she be, since the seven were married to her?"*

After declaring they knew neither the scriptures nor the power of God, Jesus responded: *"When the dead rise, they will neither marry nor be given in marriage; they will be like the angels in heaven. Now about the dead rising—have you not read in the book of Moses, in the account of the bush, how God said to him, 'I am the God of Abraham, the God of Isaac, and the God of Jacob?' He is not god of the dead, but of the living."*

Through all these schemes and clever attempts to demean and entrap Jesus, Jesus reveals knowledge of the Scriptures and significant debating skills.

## DIALOGUE

1. ***Why do you think Jesus allowed the religious leaders to play these games at his expense?***
2. ***What strikes you most about Jesus' statements about life after death?***
3. ***What are your thoughts about the resurrection of the dead? Do you believe in an afterlife?***
4. ***Do you believe you will be with loved ones after death? Will you recognize them?***
5. ***What do you think God meant when he told Moses:*** **I am the God of Abraham, the God of Isaac, and the God of Jacob.**
6. ***What do you think Jesus meant when he said*** **that God is not the god of the dead, but of the living.**
7. ***How can you relate this experience to your own life's journey?***

## JOURNAL

### 37. Do religious leaders today better understand their roles than those who stood in the way of Jesus?

Noting how deftly Jesus answered his challengers, one of the teachers of the law approached him and asked which of the commandments was the most important. *"The most important one," answered Jesus, "is this, 'Hear, O Israel, the Lord our God, the Lord is one. Love the Lord your God with all your heart and with all your soul and with all your mind and with all your strength.' The second is this 'Love your neighbor as yourself.' There is no commandment greater than these."* The teacher of the law agreed with Jesus, affirming that he was right, and added that obeying these commandments was much better than all the burnt offerings and sacrifices. Jesus told this wise man that he was not far from the kingdom of God.

This teacher of the law was not, as we might assume, asking Jesus which of the Ten Commandments was most important.

The rabbis in that day had compiled a list of 613 commandments in the Law (the Hebrew Bible—what Christians call the Old Testament): 248 were positive (things you *should* do) and 365 were negative (things you *should not* do). Jesus' answer was astounding, for "the Greek word which is translated 'love' applies to the volition rather than to the emotions, to the will rather than to the affections. Love to God manifests itself primarily in obedience. ... The religious folk of Jesus' day assumed that it was possible to love God without necessarily loving all of ones fellow men."[10]

Jesus did not give all scribes a clean bill of spiritual health, however. In fact, he cautioned his disciples and the masses about these "authorities" of religious law. *"They like to walk around in flowing robes and be greeted in the marketplaces, and have the most important seats in the synagogues and the places of honor at banquets. They devour widows' houses and for a show make lengthy prayers. Such men will be punished most severely."*

## DIALOGUE

1. ***Do you agree with Jesus and this scribe about what religious rules/commandments are most important to obey?***

2. ***What do you think led (and continues to lead) religious leaders to behave as the Pharisees, Sadducees, elders, priests, chief priests, and scribes behaved toward Jesus?***

3. ***How easy or difficult is it for you to love God with all your heart, soul, mind, and strength?***

4. ***Do you love yourself? What does Jesus mean in assuming that we love ourselves?***

5. ***How easy or difficult is it for you to love your neighbors as you love yourself?***

6. *Is it possible to love God and not love your neighbors?*

7. *How can you relate this experience to your own life's journey?*

## JOURNAL

**CHAPTER ELEVEN**

# JERUSALEM AND THE MOUNT OF OLIVES

## *Segments 38-40*

### 38. What was Jesus' view about wealth?

Jesus and his followers sat in the Temple courts by the treasury where people came to give their offerings. *Many rich people threw in large amounts. But a poor widow came and put in two very small copper coins, worth only a fraction of a penny.* Jesus observed: *"I tell you the truth, this poor widow has put more into the treasury than all the others. They all gave out of their wealth; but she, out of her poverty, put in everything—all she had to live on."*

As they were leaving the Temple, one of the disciples called their attention to the magnificent buildings constructed of massive stones. *"Do you see all these great buildings?" replied Jesus. "Not one stone here will be left on another; every one will be thrown down."*

They returned to the Mount of Olives and there, opposite the temple, Peter, James, John, and Andrew asked Jesus to clarify the signs that would signal the coming of the "last days." Jesus responded: *"Many will come in my name, proclaiming, 'I am he,' and will deceive many. When you hear of wars and rumors of wars, do not be alarmed. Such things must happen, but the end is still to come. Nation will rise against nation and kingdom against kingdom.*

*There will be earthquakes in various places, and famines. These are the beginnings of birth pains."*

## DIALOGUE

1. *If you were a reporter for the* **Jerusalem Financial Times** *assigned to interview Jesus on the topic "the meaning of money," how do you think he would answer the question? What other questions would you ask Jesus about wealth and poverty?*

2. *When Jesus spoke of the* **last days** *do you think he was referring to things yet to happen (beyond our time) or things that have already come to pass (before our time)?*

3. *How do Jesus' words on the last days strike you? Do you find them somber? To what extent do they concern you or make you think about how to live your life?*

4. *If you could interview Jesus about these words to his disciples, what would you like to ask him?*

5. *Do you see any evidence of false prophets today? If so, what?*

6. *Do you see evidence of "birth pains" today? If so, what?*

7. *How can you relate this experience to your own life's journey?*

### GROUP DIALOGUE POWER TIP

Dialogue leads to koinonia (community). With the energy of an authentic communion, dialogue leads to a sense of the "whole" and to a path to participate in that "whole." In koinonia we find a path beyond the fragments of community to community as the whole family of humankind.

## JOURNAL

**39. How do you explain the survival of what Jesus launched?**

Jesus told his disciples that the end of times would not come until the gospel (the good news) was preached to all nations. They were the agents through which this mission would be accomplished. He warned them that they would pay a price for associating with him: They would be hated, beaten, and taken to court. But he added: *"Whenever you are arrested and brought to trial, do not worry beforehand about what to say, just say whatever is given you at the time, for it is not you speaking, but the Holy Spirit. ... All men will hate you because of me, but he who stands firm to the end will be saved."*

## DIALOGUE

1. ***Put yourself in the sandals of one of the 12 disciples. How would Jesus' warning strike you? Would you continue your relationship as a disciple of Jesus? Why or why not?***

2. *If being a Christian became difficult or dangerous for you (for example, if practicing your faith were to become illegal), would you be willing to risk imprisonment or prosecution (maybe even persecution) being a disciple of Jesus Christ? Why or why not?*

3. *What level of challenge or hardship do you think you could endure as a disciple of Jesus Christ?*

4. *Are you aware of those who are persecuted for Christ in the world today? If so, who?*

5. *There is an old hymn* **Stand Up, Stand Up for Jesus.** *What does it mean to "stand up for Jesus" today?*

6. *Jesus told the disciples not to worry about what testimony they would give. Have you ever been aware of the Holy Spirit speaking through you? When? What was it like?*

7. *How can you relate this experience to your own life's journey?*

## JOURNAL

**40. What would you like to ask Jesus about this?**

In his reference to "the abomination that causes desolation" Mark includes a note to the reader: "let the reader understand." Though we are not entirely sure what Jesus was referring to, we can say for sure that this abomination that causes desolation wreaks a lot of destruction, for there is a reference to great tribulation. *"For false Christs and false prophets will appear and perform signs and miracles to deceive the elect."* The sun will be darkened, the moon will not give its light, and stars will fall from heaven. *"At that time they will see the Son of man coming in clouds with great power and glory. And he will send his angels, and gather his elect from the four winds, from the ends of the earth to the ends of the heavens."*

*"No one knows about that day or hour, not even the angels in heaven, nor the Son, but only the Father. Be on guard! Be alert!"*

The Passover and the Feast of Unleavened Bread were only two days away, and the religious leaders were looking for a way to arrest Jesus and do away with him. *"But not during the Feast," they said, "or the people may riot."*

(Passover is a very important Jewish festival. Passover commemorates God's deliverance of the Jews from Egyptian bondage, called the Exodus, under the leadership of Moses.)

## DIALOGUE

**Many have speculated about the meaning of Jesus' words on the "abomination of desolation" and the Son of Man's "coming in clouds with great power and glory." One day we will have more clarity about what they meant. In the meantime:**

1. ***What would you like to ask Jesus about these things?***

2. *The religious leaders feared a riot would ensue if they arrested and killed Jesus. What does this suggest about what the leaders thought people felt about Jesus?*

3. *How can we be on guard against false Christs and false prophets?*

4. *Where do you think false Christs and false prophets gain the power to "perform signs and miracles to deceive the elect"?*

5. *Jesus clearly said that no one knows the date or time when the Son of Man will come with great power and glory. So what do you make of those who are willing to set the day and the time for his coming?*

6. *How can we be "alert" for the coming of the abomination of desolation and the coming of the Son of Man?*

7. *How can you relate this experience to your own life's journey?*

## JOURNAL

**CHAPTER TWELVE**

# BETHANY AND THE MOUNT OF OLIVES

## *Segments 41-43*

### 41. What beautiful thing have you done for Jesus?

In the house of Simon the leper in Bethany, a woman came with a jar of expensive perfume. She opened the jar and poured the perfume on Jesus' head.

Some present were outraged at the spectacle and said: *"Why this waste of perfume? It could have been sold for more than a year's wages and the money given to the poor." And they rebuked her harshly. "Leave her alone," said Jesus. "She has done a beautiful thing to me. The poor you will always have with you, and you can help them anytime you want. But you will not always have me. She did what she could. She poured perfume on my body beforehand to prepare for my burial. I tell you the truth, wherever the gospel is preached throughout the world, what she has done will also be told, in memory of her."*

Then one of the disciples, Judas Iscariot, went to the chief priests to betray Jesus. The chief priests were pleased and promised to pay Judas for this betrayal. So he began looking for an opportunity to hand Jesus over.

## DIALOGUE

The story of the woman's anointing Jesus with expensive perfume challenges us to reflect on how we may best show respect for and pay attention to Jesus as a person.

1. *Since we are not in a position to tend to Jesus physically, how can we pay appropriate attention to Jesus as a person?*

2. *How can we show respect for Jesus today?*

3. *What difference does it make whether we show respect or disrespect for Jesus?*

4. *Was the "expensive perfume" wasted? Why do you think on this occasion Jesus didn't "buy" the argument that proceeds from the sale of the perfume could have been given to the poor? (In John's account of the event, the one who objected was Judas Iscariot, who was the treasurer of the Twelve.)*

5. *What do you think could have led Judas to betray Jesus?*

6. *Have there been times when you have (or might have) betrayed Jesus? If so, what were they?*

7. *How can you relate this experience to your own life's journey?*

## JOURNAL

## 42. Why was it necessary for Jesus to be betrayed?

On the day of the Passover meal, the disciples asked Jesus where he would like to eat the special meal. He sent two of the disciples out with instructions to find a man carrying a jar of water. They were to follow him until he entered a house and then ask the owner of the house: *"The Teacher asks: 'Where is my guest room, where I may eat the Passover with my disciples?' He will show you a large upper room, furnished and ready. Make preparations for us there."*

The two disciples followed Jesus' instructions and prepared the Passover meal according to the specific requirements for the food and wine.

As they were reclining around the table that evening, Jesus said, *"I tell you the truth, one of you will betray me—one who is eating with me." They were saddened, and one by one they said to him, "Surely not I?" "It is one of the Twelve," he replied, one who dips bread in the bowl with me. ... But woe to that man who betrays the Son of Man! It would be better for him if he had not been born."*

## DIALOGUE

1. ***Why do you suppose that, as late as the morning of the Passover when the lambs were being slaughtered for the meal, Jesus was not worried about making arrangements?***
2. ***What do you think enabled Jesus to anticipate the arrangements provided for the Passover meal?***
3. ***How do you think Jesus knew about his betrayal beforehand?***
4. ***Knowing that he would betray him, why would Jesus keep Judas around?***
5. ***Why was it necessary for Jesus to be betrayed?***
6. ***Was there any other way for Jesus to complete his mission?***
7. ***How can you relate this experience to your own life's journey?***

## JOURNAL

**43. Why did Jesus attach importance to this Passover meal?**

*While they were eating, Jesus took bread, gave thanks and broke it, and gave it to his disciples, saying, "Take it; this is my body." Then he took the cup, gave thanks and offered it to them, and they all drank from it. "This is my blood of the covenant, which is poured out for many," he said to them. "I tell you the truth, I will not drink again of the fruit of the vine until that day when I drink it anew in the kingdom of God."*

They concluded the Passover meal in the traditional way—singing a hymn.

Then they returned to the Mount of Olives and there Jesus said:

*"You will all fall away. For it is written, 'I will strike the shepherd and the sheep will be scattered.' But after I have risen, I will go ahead of you into Galilee." Peter declared, "Even if all fall away, I will not." "I tell you the truth," Jesus answered, "today—yes, tonight—before the rooster crows twice, you yourself will disown me three times." But Peter insisted emphatically, "Even if I have to die with you, I will never disown you." And all the others said the same.*

### DIALOGUE

**The Last Supper was the basis for a sacrament or ordinance in most Christian churches (communion or the Lord's supper).**

1. ***Why do you think Jesus attached such importance to this Passover meal?***

2. ***How do you account for the courage the disciples displayed in the face of the trials to come?***

3. ***Do you believe that Peter was absolutely sincere in declaring his loyalty to Jesus?***

4. *If you were tasked with writing a tell-all biography of Peter, what would a few of your chapter titles be (based on Peter's behavior in Mark's gospel)?*

5. *If you had been present at this Passover meal, what emotions would you have experienced?*

6. *If you were one of the disciples at this junction in the journey with Jesus, what would you be thinking about how to carry on in the absence of Jesus?*

7. *How can you relate this experience to your own life's journey?*

## JOURNAL

**CHAPTER THIRTEEN**

# GETHSEMANE

## *Segments 44-45*

JESUS PRAYING IN THE GARDEN

**44. What does this tell you about Jesus' relationship to God?**

Later that evening, they went out to the Garden of Gethsemane. Jesus asked the disciples to wait while he went aside to pray. He took Peter, James, and John with him and told them of his great distress: *"My soul is overwhelmed with sorrow to the point of death. Stay here, and keep watch." Going a little farther, he fell to the ground and prayed that if possible the hour might pass from him. "Abba, Father," he said, "everything is possible for you. Take this cup from me. Yet not what I will, but what you will."*

When he returned he found the disciples sleeping. *"Simon," he said to Peter, "are you asleep? Could you not keep watch for one hour? Watch and pray that you will not fall into temptation. The spirit is willing, but the body is weak." Once more he went away and prayed the same thing. When he came back, he again found them sleeping, because their eyes were heavy. They did not know what to say to him. Returning the third time, he said to them, "Are you still sleeping and resting? Enough! The hour has come. Look, the Son of Man is betrayed into the hands of sinners. Rise! Let us go! Here comes my betrayer."*

## DIALOGUE

1. ***What does the Gethsemane experience reveal about Jesus' identity and his relationship with God?***

2. ***What strikes you most about his prayer?***

3. ***What do you think accounts for Peter, James, and John's lack of discipline regarding Jesus' request for them to watch while he prayed? How did Jesus respond to finding them asleep on their watch?***

4. *If we see the humanity of Jesus and his disciples in this experience, what would you say about the power of God in each of their lives at this time?*

5. *Have there been times in your life when you have found yourself lacking in courage and discipline? If so, how did (or could) you access the power of God to strengthen you?*

6. *Have there been times in your life when your spirit was willing but your body was weak? What does it take to strengthen you at such times?*

7. *How can you relate this experience to your own life's journey?*

## JOURNAL

### 45. If you had been there, would you have fled?

Then came Judas. *With him was a crowd armed with swords and clubs, sent from the chief priests, the teachers of the law, and the elders. Now the betrayer had arranged a signal with them: "The one I kiss is the man; arrest him and lead him away under guard." Going at once to Jesus, Judas said, "Rabbi!" and kissed him. The men seized Jesus and arrested him.*

One of those standing near drew his sword and sliced off the ear of one of the high priest's servants. *"Am I leading a rebellion," said Jesus, "that you have come out with swords and clubs to capture me? Every day I was with you, teaching in the temple courts, and you did not arrest me. But the scriptures must be fulfilled." Then everyone deserted him and fled.*

## DIALOGUE

1. ***What do you think were Judas' motives in betraying Jesus? What was in it for him—really?***

2. ***Can you imagine any circumstances that might have led you to do what Judas did?***

3. ***Does it surprise you that one of the disciples carried a sword?***

4. ***What explanation does Jesus offer for his capture?***

5. ***Picture yourself there in the Garden amongst the disciples. Why do you think they deserted him and fled? If you had been there, would you have fled? Why or why not?***

6. ***What do you think happened to the disciples' courage that we saw earlier?***

7. ***How can you relate this experience to your own life's journey?***

## JOURNAL

## CHAPTER FOURTEEN

# JERUSALEM

### *Segments 46-48*

**46. How did the religious leaders come to act this way?**

The captors led Jesus to the high priest, and all the chief priests, elders, and teachers of the law assembled. Peter followed at a safe distance then sat with the guards and warmed himself by the fire.

*The chief priests and the whole Sanhedrin* [the council of priests] *were looking for false evidence against Jesus so they could put him to death. But they did not find any.* Many testified falsely against him, but their statements did not agree. After listening to some of the false witnesses, the high priest asked Jesus, *"Are you not going to answer? What is this testimony that these men are bringing against you?"* Jesus was silent. *The high priest said to him, "I charge you under oath by the living God: Tell us if you are the Christ, the Son of God." "Yes, it is as you say," Jesus replied. "But I say to all of you: In the future you will see the Son of Man sitting at the right hand of the Mighty One and coming on the clouds of heaven."* At this point, the high priest tore his garments—expressing his outrage—and asked what further evidence was necessary. He said, *"Look, now you have heard the blasphemy. What do you think?"* They all condemned Jesus as worthy of death. Some spat on him. They blindfolded him, struck him, and challenged him to prophesy. Then they handed him over to the guards who beat him.

## DIALOGUE

1. *How does this trial strike you—as just (from a purely human standpoint) or unjust? Did Jesus get a fair trial?*

2. *If you had been called as a witness for the defense (Jesus), what would you have said in his defense?*

3. *If you were appointed counsel to represent Jesus in the trial, what argument would you have made for his innocence?*

4. *Do you think any argument—however brilliantly conceived and skillfully presented—could have swayed the jury of priests to acquit Jesus?*

5. *The official verdict of guilt rested on the charge of blasphemy. What was the blasphemy for which Jesus was accused?*

6. *Jesus gives us a perfect example of doing the right thing even though it is extremely difficult. When is doing the right thing hard?*

7. *How can you relate this experience to your own life's journey?*

## JOURNAL

**47. What do you think Jesus would have said to Peter?**

While Peter was still down in the courtyard by the fire, one of the high priest's servant girls saw him and said, *"You also were with that Nazarene, Jesus." But he denied it. "I don't know or understand what you are talking about," he said, and went out into the entryway.* The servant girl followed and announced to those standing by that Peter was one of Jesus' followers. *Again he denied it. After a little while, those standing near said to Peter, "Surely you are one of them, for you are a Galilean." He began to call down curses on himself, and he swore to them, "I don't know this man you are talking about." Immediately the rooster crowed the second time. Then Peter remembered the word Jesus had spoken to him: "Before the rooster crows twice you will disown me three times." And he broke down and wept.*

## DIALOGUE

1. ***What strikes you most about Peter's denial of Jesus?***

2. ***Can you relate to what Peter must have been going through? Have you ever been in a conflicted position even remotely similar to this? If so, how did you feel?***

3. ***Can you imagine a situation in which you would deny knowing someone if*** **guilt by association** ***might mark you for punishment—or even death? If so, what would influence your decision to do so?***

4. ***What role do you think fear played in Peter's response? Why did faith not overcome Peter's fear?***

5. ***If you were Peter now and saw Jesus, what would you say to him? What would you feel?***

6. *What do you think Jesus' response would be?*

7. *Are there areas of your life in which you deny Jesus? If so, how?*

8. *How can you relate this experience to your own life's journey?*

## JOURNAL

48. **How do you think Jesus felt about this trial?**

Early the next morning, the religious leaders reached a verdict—guilty. They bound Jesus and delivered him to Pilate, the Roman governor of the region. Pilate was responsible to Rome for preserving order in his jurisdiction. *"Are you the king of the Jews?" asked Pilate. "Yes, it is as you say," Jesus replied. The chief priests accused him of many things. So again Pilate asked him, "Aren't you going to answer? See how many things they are accusing you of." But Jesus still made no reply, and Pilate was amazed.*

Each year during the Passover Festival Pilate would set free any prisoner the crowd asked for. Barabbas was a criminal in prison with a band of rebels convicted of committing a murder during a riot. (He was a Jewish nationalist—perhaps a Zealot—whose hatred of Israel's enemies may have appealed more to some Jews than Jesus' teaching to love your enemies.)

The crowd gathered to make their customary request. *"Do you want me to release to you the king of the Jews?" asked Pilate, knowing that it was out of envy that the chief priests had handed Jesus over to him. But the chief priests stirred up the crowd to have Pilate release Barabbas instead. "What shall I do, then, with the one you call the king of the Jews?" Pilate asked them. "Crucify him," they shouted. "Why? What crime has he committed?" asked Pilate. But they shouted all the louder, "Crucify him!" Wanting to satisfy the crowd, Pilate released Barabbas to them. He had Jesus flogged, and handed him over to be crucified.*

## DIALOGUE

1. ***If you were granted an interview with Pilate in the days following Jesus' trial, what questions would you ask him?***

2. ***If you asked Jesus what he was feeling during this time how do you think he would answer? What emotions do you think he would say he was feeling?***

3. ***How do you explain the role the crowd played in the drama of the arrest and conviction of Jesus?***

4. ***How susceptible are you to a "mob mentality"? Have you ever been caught up in an event of such great peer pressure? If so, how did you respond?***

5. *Have there been times when you resisted the "prevailing" sentiment to stand for what you believed was right? When? How? If not, are there times you wish you had?*

6. *If you were covering this event for the* **Jerusalem Gazette,** *what would the main points of your story be? What would your lead be?*

7. *How can you relate this experience to your own life's journey?*

## JOURNAL

**CHAPTER FIFTEEN**

# GOLGOTHA

## *Segments 49-52*

THE CRUCIFIXION

**49. How do you think Jesus felt about the soldiers who crucified him?**

Crucifixion was perhaps the most torturous form of capital punishment in human history. Our English word "excruciating" (extremely painful) comes from the root word "crux" or cross—so named from the crucifixion. The Egyptians invented it, the Persians used it, and the Greeks adopted it from the Persians. When Alexander the Great captured Tyre, he ordered the execution of 2,000 on crosses by the seashore. The Romans learned crucifixion from the Greeks and added the use of spikes and scourging to make it even more painful.

Soldiers were charged with carrying out the crucifixion of Jesus. They clothed him in a purple cloak and put a crown of thorns on his head. They mocked him with facetious salutes: "Hail, King of the Jews!" They struck his head with a reed and spat upon him. They knelt down in mock homage to him. After mocking him, they stripped him of the purple cloak and put his own clothes back on him.

They led Jesus out of town to crucify him and forced a passerby, Simon of Cyrene, to carry his cross. They brought him to Golgotha (which means the "place of a skull"). They offered him wine mixed with myrrh (as an anesthetic) but he refused to drink it. They nailed him to the cross at the third hour—nine a.m.

They divided his clothes among them and cast lots to decide what each would take. They posted the charge against him on the cross: *The King of the Jews.* Jesus was on the cross for six hours.

They crucified two robbers with him—one on his right and one on his left.

Passersby hurled insults at Jesus and shouted: "*So! You who are going to destroy the temple and rebuild it in three days, come down from the cross and save yourself!*"

The religious leaders also mocked him. *"He saved others," they said, "but he can't save himself! Let this Christ, this King of Israel, come down now from the cross, that we may see and believe."*

Darkness came over the whole land and at the ninth hour (three p.m.) Jesus cried out with a loud voice: *"Eloi, Eloi, lama sabachthani?"—which means, "My God, my God, why have you forsaken me?"* After being taunted with a sponge full of vinegar to drink, *with a loud cry, Jesus breathed his last. The curtain of the temple was torn in two from top to bottom.*

A centurion (a Roman military commander of 50–100 soldiers) who stood there in front of Jesus saw how he died and said, *"Surely this man was the Son of God!"*

## DIALOGUE

1. ***The religious leaders suggested that if Jesus were the Christ, he would come down from the cross and save himself. What would you say to the religious leaders in response to this assumption?***

2. ***What do the religious leaders' words imply about their understanding of the mission of the Messiah?***

3. ***If you asked Jesus what he meant when he said that God had forsaken him, what do you think his answer would be?***

4. ***What do you think moved the centurion to declare that Jesus must be the Son of God?***

5. ***If this was a sincere affirmation of the centurion's faith, what difference would this likely have made in his life and work?***

6. *People responded to Jesus' crucifixion in various ways (and still do today). What do you think accounts for the differences?*

7. *How can you relate this experience to your own life's journey?*

## JOURNAL

## 50. What was special about the presence of the women?

Though there was not a woman among the Twelve, women were always around Jesus during his ministry as recorded in the Gospel of Mark—Peter's mother-in-law, the woman with a flow of blood, Herodias and her daughter, the Syrophoenician woman, and the woman at Bethany who anointed his hair with oil. What's more, we see that they were willing to behave in unconventional ways. They sought him—a rabbi—for help and ministered to him.

So it is not surprising that three women—Mary Magdalene, Mary the mother of James the younger and of Joses, and Salome—witnessed Jesus' crucifixion from a distance. They had followed Jesus and cared for his needs. Many women who came up with him to Jerusalem were also there.

## DIALOGUE

1. *What do you think was remarkable about the presence of women at this gruesome event? Why do you suppose they witnessed Jesus' crucifixion from a distance?*

2. *As you review the events in Jesus' life, have you noticed any difference in the way men versus women responded to him? If so, what was the difference?*

3. *Have you noticed any difference in the way people of different socioeconomic status, ethnicity, or religious background responded to him? If so, what were the differences?*

4. *Do you think that your own gender, status, ethnicity, educational level, or religious background affects how you respond to Jesus? If so, how? If any of those things were different, how do you think your response to (and view of) Jesus might be different?*

5. *Jesus' invitation was to all people. Do you think some types of people respond to Jesus more readily than others? If so, how?*

6. *Do you think diversity makes it more or less difficult for followers of Jesus to congregate and serve him together? If so, how?*

7. *How can you relate this experience to your own life's journey?*

## JOURNAL

### 51. What was the source of the courage of Joseph of Arimathea?

Joseph of Arimathea, a respected member of the Sanhedrin who himself was waiting for the kingdom of God, mustered his courage and went to Pilate and requested the body of Jesus. Pilate granted his request. *So Joseph bought some linen cloth, took down the body, wrapped it in the linen, and placed it in a tomb cut out of a rock. Then he rolled a stone against the entrance to the tomb. Mary Magdalene and Mary the mother of Joses saw where he was laid.*

After the Sabbath, Mary Magdalene and Mary the mother of James and Salome bought spices to anoint Jesus' body. As they were on their way to the tomb just after sunrise, they asked each other how they would get the stone rolled away from the entrance to the tomb.

*But when they looked up, they saw that the stone, which was very large, had been rolled away. As they entered the tomb, they saw a young man dressed in a white robe sitting on the right side, and they were alarmed. "Don't be alarmed," he said. "You are looking for Jesus the Nazarene, who was crucified. He has risen! He is not here. See the place where they laid him. But go, tell his disciples and Peter, 'He is going ahead of you into Galilee. There you will see him, just as he told you!'" Trembling and bewildered, the women went out and fled from the tomb. They said nothing to anyone, because they were afraid.*

## DIALOGUE

1. ***What did Joseph of Arimathea—a member of the Jewish council that had convicted Jesus—risk in asking for the body of Jesus?***

2. ***Where do you think Joseph found the courage to do what he did?***

3. ***Under what circumstances would you have taken the risks that Joseph took?***

4. ***If you had taken that risk, what would have been the source of your courage?***

5. ***Have you ever taken such a risk in your faith walk?***

6. ***Why do you think the women were trembling, bewildered, and afraid?***

7. ***How can you relate this experience to your own life's journey?***

## JOURNAL

### 52. What was the Good News that Jesus wanted preached to the whole creation?

*Later Jesus appeared to the Eleven as they were eating; he rebuked them for their lack of faith and their stubborn refusal to believe those who had seen him after he had risen. He said to them, "Go into all the world and preach the good news to all creation. Whoever believes and is baptized will be saved, but whoever does not believe will be condemned."*

THE APOSTLES PREACHING THE GOSPEL

## DIALOGUE

1. *Does it surprise you that Mark (and Peter who was very likely his source for the gospel) was so "brutally honest" as to acknowledge the "lack of faith" and "stubborn refusal to believe" on the part of those closest to Jesus?*

2. *Why do you think they would be willing to let those with whom they were sharing the gospel know this?*

3. *What is your understanding of Jesus after taking this journey? What new discoveries did you make? What new insights did you gain?*

4. *Will your life be any different as a result of this journey with Jesus? If so, how?*

5. *With whom would you like to share your experience on this journey?*

6. *In this journey, have you found any new power to support your courage to be a follower of Jesus, the Anointed One, the Christ, the Messiah?*

7. *How can you relate this experience to your own life's journey?*

## JOURNAL

Though your journey with Jesus in this book has ended and your dialogue sessions are formally over, your spiritual dialogue with Jesus can go on forever. Jesus promised to transform all that follow him.

## THE APOSTLE PAUL TOOK THE GOOD NEWS TO THE GREEKS

The book of Acts picks up where Mark's gospel leaves off. In it we find Paul, a former persecutor of Christians turned apostle, spreading the gospel ("good news") throughout the Roman Empire. During a visit to a public forum in Athens, the capital city of Greece, the Apostle Paul noticed many objects of worship reflecting the religious interests of the Athenians. There was even an altar with the inscription: *To an Unknown God.* Paul used this as a basis for his witness and stated that he knew the "unknown god" and would make him known through his proclamation.

*"The God who made the world and everything in it is the Lord of heaven and earth and does not live in temples built by hands. And he is not served by human hands, as if he needed anything, because he himself gives all men life and breath and everything else. From one man he made every nation of men that they should inhabit the whole earth and he determined the times set for them and the exact places where they should live. God did this so that men would seek him and perhaps reach out for him and find him, though he is not far from each one of us.* ***For in him we live and move and have our being."***

The Acts of the Apostles 17:24–28a

# APPENDICES

## SUGGESTIONS TO OPTIMIZE GROUP DIALOGUE

True dialogue occurs when a group *becomes open to the flow of a "larger intelligence."* Deeper dialogue leads to greater discovery for all participants, and more intimate dialogue has potential for significant transformation. Dialogue releases energy, stretches, and liberates. It brings us into the realm of the eternal where we may discover profound knowledge and wisdom.

The type of dialogue we are encouraging here is not another word for *discussion* or *debate.* Discussion is analytical and typically picks things apart. In debate, sides seek to win points. Dialogue requires us to suspend assumptions and opinions to be receptive to new understanding. It leads to opening up to a bigger picture.

Have you experienced this kind of dialogue? If so, see if you can pinpoint some things that made that happen. Sometimes you realize that in the course of exploring thoughts and feelings and exchanging meaning, you feel very close to someone. You gain an important insight, discover a profound truth, or realize that a relationship has come alive. Dialogue leads to *koinonia,* a spirit of fellowship and community in which people gain energizing and durable relationships.

According to Louise Diamond, this type of dialogue intends:

- Not to advocate but to inquire
- Not to argue but to explore
- Not to convince but to discover

Instead of listening to determine who is right or what is correct or to find agreement, it is important to listen to find *what is meant*. Daniel Yankelovich put it this way:

*I do not, while talking with you, selectively tune out views I disagree with, nor do I busy myself marshaling arguments to rebut you while only half attending to what you have to say.* [11] We must engage one another's views to enhance our mutual understanding.

It is important to assume that each member of the group has a piece of the answer to a question and that, *together*, the group can craft a new and better answer. Always celebrate new insights, greater clarity, and deeper understandings when they occur. When members disclose such shifts in their thinking, they demonstrate an openness that can be contagious.

When someone's contribution is not clear, it is often helpful to restate that person's contribution in different words then check it out: "Am I getting what you mean?" Such attempts to clarify can surface new layers of meaning that go beyond the initial contribution.

Agreement is *not* the purpose of dialogue. It is important, however, to suspend judgment about others' contributions, and disagreements should be shared openly. Disagreements should be seen as a different way of looking at a subject. Disagreements can energize a group to seek meaning and clarity that goes beyond the initial conflicting views.

In dialogue there is a cool energy like that associated with a superconductor. This energy exchange allows all points of view to be expressed without either party of the exchange becoming defensive. With wasted energy diminished, hot topics can be discussed and become windows to deeper insights.

Barriers to effective dialogue:

- Ingrained habits of non-listening
- Pride that gets in the way
- Resistance to change
- Different personalities and personality types
- Disrespect for one another may suppress openness
- Lack of trust—resistance to reveal "secrets"
- Egos—would require increased vulnerability
- Competitiveness including jockeying for influence

Dialogue begins with an exchange of ideas, thoughts, and views. These exchanges lead to probing. When there is an exchange of meaning that goes beyond an exchange of words, thoughts, and views there is movement toward what Martin Buber called "I-Thou" relationships. Buber distinguished between "I-It" relationships—in which we treat one another as *objects*—and "I-Thou" relationships—in which we treat one another as *persons*. In "I-Thou" relationships, we experience an enhanced sense of alignment within ourselves and between us.

Ultimately, dialogue leads to *koinonia* (community). Fueled by the energy of an authentic communion, dialogue leads to a sense of the "whole" and to a path to participate in that "whole." Barriers come down and lives are shared. In *koinonia* we find a path beyond the fragments of community that leads to community as the whole family of humankind.

In dialogue, transformation is experienced that leads to enriched "fields" of influence, a greater sense of "the whole," and even potential encounter with *The Eternal Thou* (Buber).[12]

Throughout the journey, keep these key questions before the group:

- What was Jesus' mission?
- Who did he include in his mission?
- How did he wish his mission to be continued?
- Are you ready to participate in that mission?

## SUGGESTIONS FOR LEADERS OF DIALOGUE GROUPS

For group dialogue sessions, we recommend:

- at least seven members but not more than 12
- meetings on a weekly, bi-weekly, or monthly basis
- that group members read *THE INVITATION* prior to the first session

When you begin dialogue sessions with a group (especially if the group has not met together before), provide an orientation that includes the following:

- **Self Introductions**—Invite members to introduce themselves and share (as they are comfortable) their reasons for joining this group and their expectations.
- **Logistics**—Clarify the meeting schedule, location, preparations, and attendance expectations.
- **Overview**—Provide an overview of what is included in the book and the scope of the work and process.
- **Clarification**—Share (in your own words) the information about dialogue presented in previous appendix: Suggestions to Optimize Group Dialogue.

The ongoing role of the leader (or facilitator) is to encourage dialogue and exchange to help participants:

- Be more confident in their understanding of Jesus
- Find greater clarity for the purpose of their lives
- Be more willing to share honest thoughts and feelings
- Have more courage to share opinions that might be challenged

- Have more courage to ask questions about the Bible
- Be more effective listeners
- Value different points of view
- Be more understanding of different points of view
- Encourage others to express their points of view
- Be willing to help others clarify their points of view
- Help others participate in authentic dialogue
- Feel better about the spiritual dimension of their lives

**Some important things to keep in mind:**

Everyone in a dialogue group can contribute to discovery and group learning. Small groups provide more time and space for individual contributions, whereas larger groups provide a wider array of contributions. No one member has more authority than others (the group is a democracy). Contributions should be *personal* not *positional*—meaning they should be expressed as personal views rather than as positions of an external authority or doctrine.

Personal experiences can contribute to dialogue. However, it is important to restrict the sharing of personal experience so as not to impede the sharing of understandings, opinions, and insights. On-topic sharing can advance dialogue, but ensure that group members know that a dialogue group is not a therapy group or an informal chat session.

There are times when it is appropriate to call time-out to collectively examine how the dialogue process is going.

Questions stimulate thought. Reflective thought examines assumptions. Examined assumptions lead to deeper convictions. Deeper convictions lead to profound change. Ponder the questions raised by the events in Jesus' life.

For the facilitator, this requires:

- attentive, active listening
- making certain that different points of view are not only expressed but understood and respected
- recognizing fresh insights and encouraging the group to elaborate on them
- being willing to listen to silence for reflection and sharing at a new level
- limiting input from more dominant members and encouraging input from more reserved members
- helping the group get back on course when it strays
- celebrating breakthrough or milestone "revelations" when they occur

The facilitator may also contribute thoughts and insights but should avoid becoming a dominant leader. The facilitator of a dialogue group must be a servant leader.

**Some frequently-cited benefits of participating in a dialogue group:**

- Enjoyed exchange of ideas—good mental stimulation
- Small groups bring introverts and extroverts together
- Small groups give courage to speak and share ideas
- Sessions helped to understand self
- Questions stimulate new thought

We have learned about *dialogue* from many sources. Peter Senge, senior lecturer at M.I.T., in *The Fifth Discipline,*[13] led us to understand the critical role of *dialogue* in organizational learning. *On Dialogue,*[14] by quantum physicist David Bohm, added to our understanding of *dialogue* as a path to profound communication. Public opinion researcher Daniel Yankelovich, in *The Magic of Dialogue,*[15] affirms *dialogue* as a means to social as well as individual transformation.

## NOTES REGARDING ILLUSTRATIONS

The illustrations in this book are the works of Gustave Doré (1832-1883), an Alsatian artist who specialized in woodcut book illustrations.

The following is an excerpt from *A Biography of Gustave Doré* written by Dan Malan, also author of *Gustave Doré–Adrift on Dreams of Splendor*:

Gustave Doré (1832-83) was the most popular illustrator of all time, both in terms of number of engravings (10,000+) and number of editions (4,000+). In the 40-year period from 1860-1900 a new Doré illustrated edition was published every eight days! His 238 Bible engravings were by far the most popular set of illustrations ever done, with nearly 1,000 editions.

Gustave Doré was born in Strasbourg in January 1832. He was the ultimate child prodigy. His earliest dated drawings were from the age of five. The stories of his early artistic prowess are legendary. By the age of 12 he was carving his own lithographic stones, making sets of engravings with stories to go with them. (By the way, he never had an art lesson in his life.)

For nearly 20 years Doré would be literally the most famous artist in the world. It was often said that you could find Doré folios in every English-speaking home where they could spell the word "art." In 1867 a gallery was opened in London to display his paintings. The Doré Gallery (New Bond Street) was open continuously in London for 25 years and then it toured the U.S. The British proprietors of the Doré Gallery commissioned him to do a large religious painting, similar to one of his Bible engravings.

That began a series of enormous religious canvases for which he became famous throughout the world. They became known as the greatest collection of religious paintings in the world. The French would say, "But his paintings are really just enormous illustrations," and the British would reply, "So what?"

The common folks in the American Midwest dearly loved Doré and proceeded to break every attendance record at the Art Institute of Chicago. Daily attendance exceeded 16,000 and on the final day, over 4,000 people came through the turnstiles in the final *hour!* In eight months 1.5 million people came to see the Doré exhibition. To put that in perspective, the previous record for attendance at any U.S. art museum for an entire year had been 600,000.

Vincent van Gogh referred to Doré as an "Artist of the People" because Doré took his art directed to the masses through his literary folios. Now all Doré art is in the public domain and is reprinted all over the world. Doré sets of engravings are etched into the memory of society's collective subconscious. That is his true legacy.

The Doré illustrations were taken from the web page collection of Felix Just, S.J. On his website, Father Just states: "Since these illustrations are well over 100 years old, they are in the 'public domain' and are thus free of copyright; but since I took the trouble to scan them and make them available on the web, I would appreciate receiving appropriate credit and acknowledgements. Please credit me by name (Felix Just, S.J.), include the URL of this page (http://catholic-resources.org/Art/Dore.htm), and/or link to it from your WebPages. Thanks."

## END NOTES

[1] Frederick C. Grant, *The Interpreter's Bible—The Gospel According to St. Mark* (New York–Nashville: Abingdon–Cokesbury Press, 1951).

[2] J. Middleton Murry, *Jesus—Man of Genius* (New York: Harper & Brothers, 1926).

[3] Mary Ely Lyman, *Jesus* (New York: Association Press, 1937).

[4] William Barclay, *The Gospel of Mark* (Philadelphia: The Westminster Press, 1956).

[5] Grant, *The Interpreter's Bible—The Gospel According to St. Mark.*

[6] *Pictorial Gospel of Mark* ( New York: The American Bible Society, 1963).

[7] C.F.D. Moule, *The Cambridge Bible Commentary—The Gospel of Mark* (Cambridge: Cambridge University Press, 1965).

[8] Louise Diamond, *The Courage for Peace: Daring to Create Harmony in Ourselves and in the World* (Berkely, CA: Conari Press, 2001).

[9] Lyman, *Jesus.*

[10] Ernest Trice Thompson, *The Gospel of Mark And its Meaning for Today* (Richmond, VA: John Knox Press, 1954).

[11] Daniel Yankelovich, *The Magic of Dialogue* (New York: Simon & Schuster, 2001).

[12] M.K. Smith in his article "Martin Buber on Education" (2000), in *the encyclopedia of informal education (www.infed.org),* reflecting on Buber's view that "all real living is meeting," observed that, *"The meeting involved isn't just between two people or between someone and the world. Buber believed that 'every particular* Thou *is a glimpse through to the eternal* Thou. *In other words, each and every I-Thou relationship opens up a window to the ultimate Thou."*

[13] Peter M. Senge, *The Fifth Discipline: The Art & Practice of the Learning Organization* (New York: Doubleday, 2006).

[14] David Bohm, *On Dialogue* (London: Routledge,1996).

[15] Yankelovich, *The Magic of Dialogue.*

## ABOUT THE AUTHORS

**John C. Dannemiller**—Jack, a Christian layman, has been a participant and leader in small group Bible studies for over 30 years including Bible Study Fellowship and Bethel Bible Study. He has been a frequent guest speaker at Christian Businessmen's Breakfasts and Luncheons. Dannemiller served 40 years in the corporate world, and was Chairman and CEO of a NYSE company, AIT. He was a guest lecturer at the Weatherhead Graduate Business School of Case Western Reserve University on the topics of leadership, ethics, and core values. He has served on the Boards of major corporations, banks, hospitals, non-profits, foundations, and Christian ministries. He and his wife Jean have two children, four grandchildren, and are residents of Sanibel, Florida.

## ABOUT THE AUTHORS

**Irving R. Stubbs**—Irving is an ordained Presbyterian Minister (retired) with extensive seminary training in the Scriptures. He has led many small group studies. He is a recognized leader in the implementation of the Dialogue process for small group sessions. Stubbs is co-founder of the Values Institute of America—www.valuesinstitute.org and the managing partner of Values Count, LLC. He created The Value Minute®—www.thevalueminute.com, a syndicated feature. He is the author of books and professional articles. He consults with major public and private corporations and law firms on issues including leadership, teambuilding, organizational dynamics, quality practices, ethics, and values. Irving and his wife, Ann, have five children and seven grandchildren. They reside at Westminster-Canterbury, a retirement community in Richmond, Virginia.

## EPILOGUE

In the books that follow *The Invitation* in this series, you will be able to journey with other significant personalities in the Bible whom God used to accomplish his purposes and bring about his kingdom—Paul, Moses, and Hosea the prophet. You will come to know them in fresh and enlightening ways that will surprise and encourage you to live life to the fullest. They were real people, imperfect and challenged, but in their weaknesses God demonstrated his power. As you journey with them your life will be changed as surely as their lives were changed—for the better and forever!

## THE LIVING DIALOGUE SERIES

***THE INVITATION***

In *Dialogue* with Jesus

As we know him in the Gospel of Mark

***THE JOURNEY***

In *Dialogue* with Paul

As we know him in his Letter to the Romans

***THE LAW***

In *Dialogue* with Moses

As we know him in The Book of Exodus

***THE MARRIAGE***

In *Dialogue* with Hosea

As we know him in The Prophet Hosea

***THE TRANSFORMATION***

In *Dialogue* with Jesus

As we know him in the Gospel according to John

## ABOUT VALUES COUNT, LLC.

*We seek to illumine the way to be the people God created us to be.*
This is our mission.

- We believe God calls us to think for ourselves about our choices and relationships and that dialogue is a spiritually-enriched vehicle to ground and guide that thinking.
- We affirm that it is not a new religion or religious institutions we need—but—more of us transformed by the power of the infinite, eternal and living God.
- We believe many want to be the people God created us to be. A few dilute and mislead the many toward ends and means not congruent with God's intentions. Transformed believers are challenged to energize the "multitude" with clarity of direction and the moral courage to be and act as God calls us to be and act.
- As we are transformed by the power of God, we become agents for the transformation of the communities of which we are members.
- We agree with William Penn that, *True religion shows its influence in every part of our conduct. It is like the sap of a living tree, which penetrates the most distant boughs.*

In support of these principles, Values Count, LLC. publishes books and provides media content.

Visit our website: www.valuescount.com